# SAMUEL MOORE, PSYD

# Understanding the Why Behind Our Actions

## The Hidden Motivations That Drive Us

# Contents

# Understanding the Why Behind Our Actions

Samuel Moore, PsyD

# Table of Contents

# Putting It All Together



# Appendix

# Introduction: Understanding Human Behavior

Human behavior is a fascinating and complex subject. We all act in different ways, sometimes without fully understanding why we do what we do. At the core of our actions are countless influences—biological, psychological, and social factors that shape who we are and how we interact with the world. By exploring the foundations of human behavior, we can begin to unravel the mystery behind our actions and gain valuable insight into ourselves and others.

## Why We Act the Way We Do

Our actions are driven by an intricate blend of emotions, thoughts, experiences, and instincts. From the way we make decisions to the way we respond to challenges, understanding human behavior requires an exploration of these various influences. Our upbringing, personal experiences, cultural background, and even the biological wiring of our brain all play a role in shaping our behavior.

For example, consider a situation where someone becomes defensive during a conversation. This response might stem from past experiences, fear of being judged, or a deep-seated desire to protect oneself from criticism. In this case, it's not just the immediate interaction at hand, but a combination of past memories, personality traits, and external factors that influence how they react. In understanding why we act the way we do, we can start to see patterns that help us navigate our own responses and those of others.

## The Role of Personality in Shaping Our Actions

One of the key elements in understanding human behavior is the role of personality. Personality refers to the individual differences in characteristic patterns of thinking, feeling, and behaving. It's a combination of traits that determine how we respond to different situations. Whether you're someone who's naturally introverted, someone who thrives in social settings, or someone with a high degree of empathy, your personality can dictate how you interact with others and perceive the world.

Psychologists have developed different theories to explain personality, with one of the most popular being the Big Five Personality Traits model. This framework breaks personality down into five main dimensions: openness to experience, conscientiousness, extraversion, agreeableness, and neuroticism. These traits can explain everything from your level of curiosity to your ability to manage stress. Understanding where you fall on these scales can provide you with a clearer sense of why you make the choices you do and how you can improve your interactions with others.

## How This Book Can Help You Understand Yourself and Others

This book is designed to guide you through the process of understanding human behavior on a deeper level. It will offer insights into the factors that shape actions, including the role of personality, emotions, and external circumstances. By providing a framework for recognizing behavioral patterns in yourself and others, you will be better equipped to manage relationships, make more informed decisions, and understand the driving forces behind your own behavior.

Whether you're looking to improve your communication skills, gain better self-awareness, or simply learn how to relate more effectively to those around you, this book offers practical advice and thought-provoking insights. By the end, you'll not only have a better understanding of why you act the way you do, but also the tools to interact more mindfully with others—leading to stronger connections and more meaningful interactions.

# Chapter 1: The Foundation of Human Behavior

## The Science of Behavior

Understanding behavior is not just about observing what people do—it's about digging into the underlying processes that drive those actions. The science of behavior is a multidisciplinary field that combines insights from psychology, neuroscience, biology, and sociology to explain why we think, feel, and act the way we do. By breaking down these processes, scientists have been able to develop theories and models that offer a clearer picture of how behavior works.

## The Brain and Behavior

The brain is the command center of the body, and its structure and function are crucial to understanding behavior. The brain controls every aspect of our actions, from basic reflexes to complex thoughts and emotions. Different areas of the brain are responsible for different functions. For example, the prefrontal cortex helps us with decision-making, problem-solving, and impulse control, while the amygdala is involved in processing emotions like fear and anger. These areas, among many others, work together to guide our responses to various stimuli and situations.

Neuroscience research has also uncovered how neurotransmitters—chemical messengers in the brain—play a key role in regulating mood, motivation, and behavior. For example, dopamine is linked to pleasure and reward, serotonin affects mood regulation, and Oxycontin is associated with social bonding. When the balance of these chemicals is disrupted, it can have a significant impact on behavior, often contributing to conditions like depression, anxiety, or addiction.

## Genetics and Behavior

Genetics also plays a role in shaping behavior. From an evolutionary perspective, certain behaviors may have developed as survival mechanisms. For example, the fight-or-flight response, which is triggered when we perceive danger, is an automatic reaction that has helped humans survive in threatening situations for thousands of years.

At the genetic level, research in behavioral genetics has shown that certain traits and tendencies are inherited. Twin and adoption studies, for instance, have helped scientists identify the role of genetics in personality, intelligence, and even the likelihood of developing mental health disorders. However, genetics alone doesn't determine behavior. Environmental factors also play a significant role, and the interaction between genes and the environment is what ultimately shapes individual actions.

## Environmental Influences on Behavior

While biology provides the foundation for behavior, the environment plays a critical role in shaping how we act. Our environment includes everything from the family and culture we are born into, to the people we interact with, and the broader social and cultural influences we encounter throughout our lives.

For example, social learning theory, a key concept in psychology, suggests that we learn behaviors through observation and imitation. If a child grows up in an environment where aggression is frequently modeled by parents or peers, they may be more likely to exhibit aggressive behavior themselves. Similarly, our environment influences our values, beliefs, and attitudes, all of which affect how we interpret and respond to various situations.

The environment also includes our physical surroundings. Studies have shown that factors like stress, pollution, and even the colors and layout of a room can influence our behavior. For example, research has found that people are more likely to engage in aggressive behavior in crowded environments or places with high levels of noise. On the flip side, environments that are calm and peaceful tend to promote relaxation and cooperation.

## Learning and Conditioning

One of the foundational theories in the science of behavior is the concept of conditioning. Classical conditioning, first developed by Ivan Pavlov, explains how we learn to associate certain stimuli with specific responses. In one of Pavlov's famous experiments, he trained dogs to salivate at the sound of a bell by repeatedly pairing the sound with the presentation of food. This type of learning is automatic and involuntary, and it helps explain how we develop certain emotional and behavioral reactions.

Operand conditioning, developed by B.F. Skinner, builds on this by focusing on how behavior is shaped by rewards and punishments. When behaviors are followed by positive reinforcement (a reward), they are more likely to be repeated. Conversely, if behaviors are followed by punishment or negative reinforcement, they are less likely to occur. This theory is often used in behavior therapy and is fundamental in shaping behaviors in both humans and animals.

## Cognitive Processes and Behavior

Another key factor in understanding behavior is cognition—how we think and process information. Cognitive psychology focuses on the mental processes that underlie decision-making, problem-solving, and other actions. According to cognitive theories, our thoughts and perceptions influence how we behave. For example, someone who perceives a situation as threatening may react with anxiety or aggression, while someone who views the same situation as manageable may remain calm.

Cognitive behavioral therapy (CBT) is an example of how these principles are applied to help people change negative patterns of thought that contribute to undesirable behaviors. By altering the way we think about a situation, we can change how we feel and, ultimately, how we act. This underscores the importance of self-awareness and mental habits in shaping our behavior.

## Social and Cultural Factors

Humans are social creatures, and our behavior is heavily influenced by the groups we belong to and the cultural norms we are raised with. Social psychology explores how we interact with others and how our behaviors are influenced by social situations. Concepts like conformity, obedience, and group think demonstrate how people often adjust their behavior to fit in with others or follow the lead of an authority figure, even if it goes against their personal beliefs.

Cultural factors also play a major role in shaping behavior. Every culture has its own set of norms, values, and customs that dictate how people should behave. For example, in some cultures, individualism is highly valued, leading people to prioritize personal goals and achievements, while in others, collectivism takes precedence, and group harmony is emphasized. These cultural differences shape how people approach relationships, work, and even decision-making.

## Behavioral Disorders and Mental Health

Understanding the science of behavior is also crucial for recognizing and treating behavioral disorders and mental health issues. Conditions like anxiety, depression, and personality disorders are often linked to imbalances in brain chemistry, dysfunctional thought patterns, and unhealthy environmental influences. By studying the science of behavior, therapists and counselors are better equipped to design interventions that help individuals manage and change manipulative behaviors.

In addition to therapy, modern neuroscience continues to reveal new treatments for behavioral disorders, such as medications that target specific neurotransmitters or deep brain stimulation for severe cases. These advancements highlight the ongoing progress in the field of behavioral science and its potential for improving mental health.

# Nature vs. Nurture: What Influences Our Actions?

The age-old debate of nature versus nurture has captivated psychologists, scientists, and philosophers for centuries. At its core, this debate is concerned with the relative contributions of genetic inheritance (nature) and environmental factors (nurture) to human behavior. Are our actions primarily shaped by our biological makeup, or do the experiences and influences we encounter throughout our lives play a more significant role? To answer this question, we must examine the intricate relationship between both nature and nurture and how they interact to influence who we are and how we behave.

# The Role of Nature: Genetic Inheritance and Biology

When we talk about nature's influence on behavior, we're primarily referring to the biological and genetic factors that shape who we are. From the moment of conception, we inherit a unique set of genes that influence everything from our physical traits to our psychological tendencies. Our genetic makeup provides the blueprint for our brain structure, hormone levels, and even some aspects of our personality. This biological foundation plays a critical role in shaping how we respond to the world around us.

## Genetics and Personality

Research has shown that personality traits, such as extraversion or introversion, can have a genetic basis. Twin studies, particularly those involving identical twins raised apart, have demonstrated that people who share the same genetic makeup tend to exhibit similar behaviors, even when raised in different environments. For example, studies have found that identical twins are more likely to have similar tendencies toward aggression, sociability, or impulsivity than fraternal twins, who share only half of their genetic material. This suggests that genetic factors can influence our inherent temperament and predisposition toward certain behaviors.

## The Influence of the Brain

The brain is perhaps the most direct link between nature and behavior. Different areas of the brain are responsible for processing emotions, controlling impulses, and making decisions. For example, the amygdala plays a key role in processing fear and aggression, while the prefrontal cortex is involved in decision-making and impulse control. Variations in brain structure or chemistry can influence how we react to stress, regulate our emotions, or even how we learn.

One well-known example of nature's impact on behavior is the influence of neurotransmitters like serotonin, dopamine, and norepinephrine. These chemicals regulate mood, pleasure, and arousal. When there is an imbalance in these chemicals, it can lead to mental health conditions such as depression, anxiety, or addiction. Studies have shown that some people may be genetically predisposed to these conditions, suggesting that biological factors can play a significant role in shaping behavior and emotional responses.

## Instincts and Evolutionary Influences

From an evolutionary perspective, many behaviors that we consider "natural" are deeply rooted in our biological inheritance. Instincts—innate, unlearned behaviors that occur automatically in response to certain stimuli—are hardwired into our biology. For example, the fight-or-flight response is an instinctual reaction to perceived danger, designed to increase our chances of survival. Similarly, nurturing behaviors in parents, like feeding and protecting their offspring, are rooted in evolutionary mechanisms designed to ensure the survival of the species.

Evolutionary psychology also explores how certain behaviors may have developed as adaptive responses to environmental challenges faced by our ancestors. Traits such as aggression, fear, or cooperation may have evolved to help humans navigate social structures, defend against threats, or build strong family units. Even today, some of these evolutionary influences can still be seen in the way we behave in social and stressful situations.

## The Role of Nurture: Environmental and Social Influences

While nature provides the biological blueprint, nurture involves the influences of our environment—everything from our upbringing and childhood experiences to cultural norms and social interactions. The environment in which we grow up can have a profound impact on shaping our behaviors, attitudes, and beliefs. These influences can either reinforce or challenge the innate tendencies we inherit.

## Parenting and Early Childhood Experiences

One of the most significant aspects of nurture is parenting. The way we are raised, the values instilled in us, and the emotional support we receive during childhood can heavily influence our behaviors later in life. Parenting styles—authoritative, authoritarian, permissive, or neglectful—affect a child's sense of self-worth, independence, and social competence. For example, children raised in authoritative households, where parents are nurturing yet firm, tend to develop higher self-esteem, emotional regulation, and social skills compared to those raised in authoritarian or neglectful environments.

Early childhood experiences also shape our emotional responses and cognitive patterns. For instance, children who experience consistent love and safety are more likely to develop secure attachments, which lead to positive interpersonal relationships and better emotional regulation in adulthood. Conversely, children who experience neglect or trauma may develop insecure attachments, which can contribute to emotional challenges and difficulty in forming healthy relationships later in life.

## Socialization and Peer Influence

Beyond the family, social interactions play a huge role in shaping behavior. From the moment we are born, we are social beings, influenced by our peers, teachers, and the broader community. As we grow, the social groups we belong to—such as friends, schools, workplaces, and even online communities—impact how we think, feel, and act.

Peer influence is especially significant during adolescence. During this time, individuals are forming their identities, and the behavior of friends or social groups can have a strong influence on attitudes and actions. For example, adolescents are more likely to engage in risky behavior if their friends are doing the same. This phenomenon can be explained by the desire to fit in or gain approval from others, a powerful motivator in human behavior. Social norms, whether related to fashion, morality, or behavior, often shape how we act to maintain acceptance within a group.

# Cultural Influence on Behavior

Culture is another key factor in shaping behavior. Each culture has its own set of values, norms, and expectations, which guide how people are expected to behave. Cultural influences can dictate everything from how we express emotions to how we resolve conflicts. For example, in individualistic cultures, people are often encouraged to prioritize personal goals and self-expression, while in collectivist cultures, the emphasis is more on group harmony and conformity.

Cultural practices also influence our emotional responses. In some cultures, people are taught to suppress their emotions to maintain social harmony, while in others, emotional expression is encouraged as a sign of authenticity and connection. These cultural differences shape not only how we behave in public but also how we perceive and interact with others in private.

# Socioeconomic Status and Environment

Socioeconomic status (SES) also has a significant impact on behavior. People from different socioeconomic backgrounds often have different access to resources, education, and opportunities, which can influence their behavior and life outcomes. For example, individuals from lower SES backgrounds may face more stress due to financial instability, which can affect mental health and coping mechanisms. Additionally, limited access to quality education and social services can impact a person's decision-making, career choices, and overall lifestyle.

The physical environment also plays a role. Growing up in a neighborhood with high levels of crime or instability can lead to behaviors related to survival, such as aggression or distrust. On the other hand, growing up in a supportive, well-resourced environment can encourage behaviors such as cooperation, community involvement, and optimism.

## The Interaction Between Nature and Nurture

While nature and nurture each contribute to human behavior, it is their interaction that truly shapes who we are. Both factors are not independent of one another; instead, they work in tandem. A person's genetic predispositions may make them more susceptible to certain behaviors, but their environment can either strengthen or modify those tendencies.

For example, a person with a genetic predisposition for high intelligence may thrive in an intellectually stimulating environment, such as one with access to books, educational resources, and supportive mentors. In contrast, the same person, if raised in a less stimulating environment, may not fully reach their cognitive potential, despite their genetic advantages.

Similarly, a person with a genetic predisposition to anxiety may be more sensitive to stress, but if they are raised in an environment that provides emotional support and coping strategies, they may be able to manage their anxiety more effectively.

Ultimately, it is the dynamic interplay between nature and nurture that makes us who we are. Both elements work together to shape our behavior, and understanding their influence can help us make sense of the complex ways in which we act and interact with the world around us.

## The Psychological and Biological Basis of Personality

Personality is the combination of traits, behaviors, and emotional patterns that make each individual unique. It shapes how we interact with others, respond to stress, approach challenges, and form relationships. The study of personality is complex, and understanding its origins requires looking at both psychological and biological influences. Together, these factors provide insight into why we think, feel, and behave in certain ways.

# Psychological Basis of Personality

The psychological aspect of personality revolves around the mental processes, thought patterns, and emotional experiences that shape who we are. Psychological theories of personality seek to explain how individuals develop unique characteristics based on their experiences, motivations, and interactions with the world.

## 1. Psycho dynamic Theories (Freud's Contribution)

Sigmund Freud's psychoanalytic theory was one of the earliest to propose a framework for understanding personality. According to Freud, personality is shaped by unconscious forces and early childhood experiences. He identified three components of personality:

- **The Id**: The id represents our primal desires and drives. It operates based on the pleasure principle, seeking immediate gratification of basic needs and impulses (like hunger, sex, and aggression).
- **The Ego**: The ego is the rational part of the personality that mediates between the desires of the id and the demands of the external world. It operates based on the reality principle and helps us make decisions that are socially acceptable and practical.
- **The Superego**: The superego represents our moral conscience, incorporating societal rules and cultural norms. It strives for perfection and causes feelings of guilt when we deviate from moral guidelines.

Freud believed that the balance between these three elements determines an individual's behavior and personality traits. While Freud's ideas have been widely criticized and revised, they laid the foundation for understanding the deep-seated psychological forces that influence personality.

## 2. Trait Theories

Trait theory, developed by psychologists like Gordon Allport and Raymond Cattell, focuses on identifying and measuring the stable characteristics that make up personality. These traits are consistent over time and across different situations. For instance, people who are generally outgoing and sociable tend to exhibit these behaviors in various contexts.

One of the most widely accepted trait models is the **Big Five Personality Traits** or **Five-Factor Model (FFM)**, which includes:

- **Openness to Experience**: The extent to which an individual is imaginative, curious, and open to new ideas.
- **Conscientiousness**: The degree of organization, dependability, and self-discipline.
- **Extroversion**: How outgoing, energetic, and sociable a person is.
- **Agreeableness**: The extent to which a person is cooperative, empathetic, and trusting.
- **Neuroticism**: The tendency to experience negative emotions like anxiety, sadness, and irritability.

These traits are considered to be universal dimensions of personality and have been shown to influence a wide range of behaviors, from work performance to social interactions. They provide a comprehensive framework for understanding individual differences and how they affect behavior.

## 3. Humanistic Theories

Humanistic psychology, popularized by theorists such as Carl Rogers and Abraham Maslow, emphasizes the importance of personal growth, self-actualization, and free will in shaping personality. According to humanistic theorists, personality develops as individuals strive to fulfill their potential and achieve self-acceptance.

Carl Rogers introduced the concept of the **self-concept**, which refers to how we perceive ourselves. A healthy self-concept, built on unconditional positive regard (acceptance without judgment), leads to higher self-esteem and psychological well-being. Abraham Maslow's hierarchy of needs posited that individuals are motivated by a series of needs, with self-actualization (reaching one's fullest potential) at the top. According to this theory, personality is shaped by the fulfillment of these needs, with those who reach the top of the pyramid exhibiting more harmonious, fulfilled personalities.

## Biological Basis of Personality

While psychological theories offer valuable insights into how our personality is shaped by experiences, biological influences are equally important in determining how we think, feel, and behave. These biological factors range from our genetic makeup to the structure and function of our brain, and they influence the traits and tendencies that we exhibit throughout our lives.

### 1. Genetics and Heredity

One of the most significant biological influences on personality is genetics. Research in behavioral genetics suggests that many personality traits are inherited, meaning that we may be born with a genetic predisposition for certain characteristics. Twin studies, in particular, have been instrumental in exploring the role of genetics in personality. Identical twins, who share 100% of their genetic material, tend to show remarkable similarities in traits such as extraversion, neuroticism, and conscientiousness, even when raised in different environments. In contrast, fraternal twins, who share only 50% of their genes, are less similar in personality.

Studies have shown that genes influence the neurotransmitters in our brain—such as serotonin, dopamine, and norepinephrine—which affect mood, emotional responses, and behavior. For example, a gene variation related to the serotonin transporter has been linked to higher levels of anxiety and neuroticism. Other research suggests that variations in the dopamine system may contribute to traits like extraversion and sensation-seeking behavior.

### 2. The Role of the Brain

Brain structure and function play a crucial role in shaping personality. Neuroscientific research has revealed that different regions of the brain are responsible for processing emotions, regulating behavior, and managing cognitive functions, all of which contribute to personality traits.

- **The Prefrontal Cortex**: This area of the brain is involved in decision-making, self-control, and social behavior. Damage to the prefrontal cortex can lead to impulsivity, poor decision-making, and difficulties with emotional regulation, which can affect personality.
- **The Amygdala**: The amygdala is involved in processing emotions like fear, anger, and pleasure. Its activity is linked to emotional reactivity and can influence traits like neuroticism or emotional stability. People with a more active amygdala may be more prone to anxiety or emotional distress.
- **The Striatum**: The striatum is part of the brain's reward system and is involved in processing motivation, pleasure, and reward. It is closely linked to traits like sensation-seeking, novelty-seeking, and impulsivity, which are key components of personality.

Brain imaging studies have shown that individual differences in the size, activity, and connectivity of these regions can explain variations in personality traits. For instance, research suggests that people who score high on traits like openness to experience and extraversion may have a more active prefrontal cortex and striatum, leading them to be more curious, social, and adventurous.

### 3. Hormonal Influences

Hormones also play a significant role in shaping personality. Testosterone, for example, is linked to traits such as aggression, dominance, and risk-taking. High levels of testosterone may influence behaviors associated with competitiveness and assertiveness. On the other hand, oxytocin, often referred to as the "bonding hormone," is associated with nurturing behaviors, empathy, and social bonding. People with higher oxytocin levels may be more agreeable, compassionate, and connected to others.

Hormonal fluctuations, especially during critical life stages such as adolescence, pregnancy, and menopause, can influence personality traits. For instance, during adolescence, rising levels of sex hormones like estrogen and testosterone contribute to the development of traits like increased independence, sexual identity, and emotional regulation.

## Interaction Between Psychology and Biology

Personality is shaped not only by biological factors but also by psychological experiences. These two realms—nature and nurture—are not mutually exclusive. Rather, they interact and influence each other in a complex way. For instance, a person might have a genetic predisposition toward being introverted, but if they grow up in an environment that encourages social interaction and positive reinforcement, they may develop more extraverted behaviors.

Similarly, individuals may be born with a biological tendency toward anxiety or emotional instability (due to genetic or neurological factors), but their early childhood experiences, family environment, and social support can play a key role in shaping how they cope with stress and regulate their emotions. This ongoing interplay between biology and psychology highlights the importance of considering both factors when studying personality development.

# Chapter 2: The Four Basic Personality Types

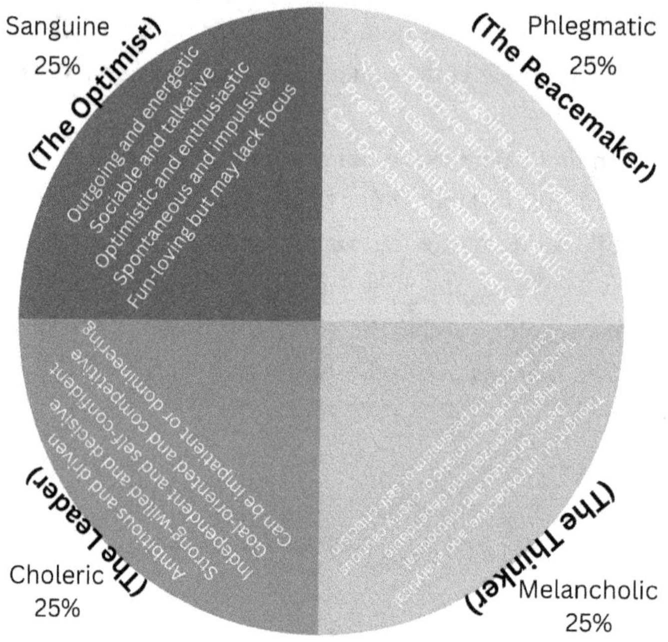


Throughout history, psychologists and thinkers have sought to understand the variety of human behaviors, leading to the development of various personality theories. One of the earliest and most enduring models is the theory of four distinct personality types, based on the idea that people exhibit certain core traits or tendencies that influence how they respond to the world. This model, originally proposed by the ancient Greek physician Hippocrates, has been refined and adapted over time but remains a useful tool for understanding human behavior.

The concept of the four personality types is rooted in the idea that individuals can be categorized into one of four basic types, each with its own set of dominant characteristics. These types—often associated with the four humors—offer a simple yet effective framework for understanding differences in how people think, feel, and act.

While modern psychology tends to focus on more complex models like the Big Five Personality Traits, the four personality types remain a popular and accessible way to discuss personality. Understanding these types can help you gain better insight into your own behavior, as well as improve interactions with others by recognizing their personality traits and tendencies.

# The Four Personality Types

# Sanguine (The Optimist)

Sanguine individuals are known for their outgoing, sociable, and cheerful nature. They are often the life of the party, drawing others in with their energy, enthusiasm, and humor. People with a sanguine personality type are generally optimistic, enjoy socializing, and are emotionally expressive. They are spontaneous, quick to laugh, and enjoy being the center of attention.

Sanguine individuals tend to be extroverted, which means they draw energy from being around others. They thrive in social situations and often excel in environments where they can engage with new people or entertain others. While they can be very fun-loving and optimistic, they may sometimes struggle with staying focused on tasks or following through with responsibilities, as they tend to seek immediate gratification.

Key traits of the **sanguine personality**:

- Outgoing and energetic

- Sociable and talkative
- Optimistic and enthusiastic
- Spontaneous and impulsive
- Fun-loving but may lack focus

# Choleric (The Leader)

Choleric personalities are driven, goal-oriented, and assertive. They are natural-born leaders who are highly motivated to achieve success and make things happen. People with a choleric personality tend to be decisive, ambitious, and independent, often taking charge in situations that require action or direction. They thrive in challenging environments and are unafraid to confront obstacles head-on.

While choleric individuals excel in leadership and achievement, they can sometimes be seen as overly aggressive or domineering. They are not afraid to take risks and may sometimes come across as impatient with others, especially if they perceive a lack of progress or efficiency. Their determination and drive can inspire those around them, but they may also push too hard for perfection.

Key traits of the **choleric personality**:

- Ambitious and driven
- Strong-willed and decisive
- Independent and self-confident
- Goal-oriented and competitive
- Can be impatient or domineering

# Melancholic (The Thinker)

Melancholic individuals are introspective, analytical, and detail-oriented. They are often deep thinkers who value accuracy and precision in their work and personal lives. People with a melancholic personality tend to be highly organized, thoughtful, and focused on quality over quantity. They prefer solitude or small, close-knit groups and often find comfort in routine and structure.

While melancholic types are excellent at critical thinking, problem-solving, and planning, they can sometimes become overly perfectionistic or bogged down by negative thoughts. They may struggle with self-doubt or pessimism, and their tendency to overanalyze situations can lead to indecision or worry. Despite this, they are loyal and dependable, often striving to make the world around them better through careful consideration.

Key traits of the **melancholic personality**:

- Thoughtful, introspective, and analytical
- Detail-oriented and methodical
- Highly organized and dependable
- Tends to be perfectionistic or overly cautious
- Can be prone to pessimism or self-criticism

# Phlegmatic (The Peacemaker)

Phlegmatic personalities are calm, easygoing, and diplomatic. They are known for their ability to remain composed in stressful situations and are often seen as the peacemakers of a group. People with a phlegmatic personality tend to be patient, considerate, and empathetic. They value harmony and are skilled at resolving conflicts and mediating between opposing viewpoints.

While phlegmatic individuals are supportive and dependable, they can sometimes be seen as passive or unassertive. They prefer to avoid conflict and may struggle to make decisions or take bold action when needed. However, their calm and peaceful nature makes them excellent listeners and friends, and they are often able to maintain stable relationships because of their accommodating nature.

Key traits of the **phlegmatic personality**:

- Calm, easygoing, and patient
- Supportive and empathetic
- Strong conflict resolution skills
- Prefers stability and harmony
- Can be passive or indecisive

## The Interaction Between the Four Personality Types

Though each of these personality types can be identified individually, it's important to remember that most people do not fit neatly into just one category. Rather, individuals may exhibit a combination of traits from different types, with one or two traits being more dominant. For example, someone might have a choleric drive to achieve success but also exhibit melancholic tendencies toward introspection and perfectionism.

Moreover, the different types often interact with one another in distinct ways. For example, a sanguine person might find the reserved, structured approach of a melancholic person intriguing but may feel frustrated by their perfectionism. Conversely, a choleric leader might clash with a phlegmatic individual who prefers to avoid conflict and take a more laid-back approach to challenges.

Understanding these personality types can help improve communication and collaboration by fostering an appreciation for different perspectives. Recognizing the inherent strengths and challenges of each type can lead to more effective teamwork, deeper relationships, and a greater sense of mutual respect.

## Using the Four Personality Types for Self-Awareness and Personal Growth

The concept of the four personality types is a helpful tool for self-awareness and personal development. By understanding which traits dominate your personality, you can gain insight into your natural tendencies and how they affect your actions, relationships, and decision-making. This knowledge can also help you identify areas for growth, such as learning to be more assertive if you're phlegmatic or managing impulsivity if you're sanguine.

Furthermore, understanding the personality types of others can improve your interactions with family, friends, colleagues, and even strangers. By adapting your communication style to suit the needs of those around you, you can build stronger, more harmonious relationships and create a positive impact on those you interact with.

In the end, the four personality types provide a simple, yet powerful, framework for understanding the diverse ways people experience and navigate the world. Whether you're looking to improve self-awareness, foster better relationships, or develop personal growth, knowing the basic types of personality is a valuable starting point.

## Sanguine: (The Social Butterfly)

The sanguine personality is often referred to as "the social butterfly" due to its outgoing, talkative, and energetic nature. People with a sanguine personality are typically extroverted, meaning they feel energized and motivated by social interactions and being around other people. They are naturally drawn to social gatherings and thrive in environments where they can connect with others, share stories, and create lively experiences. Their cheerful and optimistic disposition makes them approachable, and they often have an infectious enthusiasm that attracts others.

# Key Characteristics of Sanguine Personality

1. **Outgoing and Sociable** Sanguines are the life of the party. They are outgoing, confident, and enjoy being around others. Whether at a social gathering, a work event, or even in casual situations, they are often the first to strike up a conversation, make others laugh, and keep the mood light. Their ability to engage and connect with a wide range of people is one of their defining traits. Their extroversion helps them navigate social situations with ease and confidence, making them well-liked by many.

2. **Energetic and Enthusiastic** Sanguine individuals are full of energy and are often described as vibrant, bubbly, and animated. They tend to approach life with enthusiasm and a sense of adventure. This energy is not only physical but also emotional—sanguines are typically upbeat and optimistic about life. They are quick to see the positive side of things, and their enthusiasm often motivates and lifts the spirits of those around them.

3. **Talkative and Expressive** One of the most recognizable traits of a sanguine personality is their ability to talk and share their thoughts openly. They are expressive and often enjoy storytelling, making even mundane topics seem entertaining. They can engage in conversations with ease and often dominate discussions, sharing personal anecdotes, jokes, and insights. Their communication style is energetic, which can make them the center of attention in social settings.

4. **Spontaneous and Fun-Loving** Sanguines are spontaneous and thrive on excitement. They enjoy seeking out new experiences and are always up for a fun adventure, often without much planning. Whether it's going on an impromptu trip, trying a new activity, or making last-minute plans, they embrace the moment and look for joy in every situation. This impulsiveness is part of their charm, as they bring a sense of fun and excitement to their interactions with others.

5. **Optimistic and Positive** One of the most defining aspects of the sanguine personality is their unwavering optimism. They have a tendency to focus on the bright side of life, often ignoring the negatives or downplaying challenges. This optimism is contagious, as they can easily lift the spirits of others and encourage them to see things in a positive light. Sanguines are often quick to offer words of encouragement and are known for their "glass half full" attitude toward life.

6. **Affectionate and Caring** Despite their outgoing and sometimes larger-than-life persona, sanguines are also deeply affectionate. They enjoy forming close, personal connections with others and often express their feelings openly. Their warmth and emotional expressiveness make them easy to bond with, and they are typically very affectionate with their friends and loved ones. They are generous with their attention and like to make others feel special and valued.

7. **Easily Distracted** While sanguines' energy and enthusiasm are often seen as assets, they can also be a double-edged sword. Due to their spontaneous nature and love for novelty, they can sometimes struggle with focus and consistency. Sanguines may start many projects but have difficulty following through, often losing interest once the initial excitement fades. Their desire for new experiences can sometimes lead to a lack of attention to detail, or a tendency to jump from one interest to another without finishing what they started.

8. **Difficulty with Routine** Sanguines thrive in dynamic and fast-paced environments, but they may struggle with routines or repetitive tasks. The idea of a predictable, structured schedule can feel stifling to them. They prefer variety and excitement, which means they might find tasks that require persistence, focus, or attention to detail less enjoyable. This can make them prone to procrastination or avoidance of less stimulating activities, especially if they do not see immediate rewards or gratification.

9. **People-Oriented** At their core, sanguines are people-oriented individuals. They derive much of their energy and sense of self from

interactions with others. Whether they're engaging in casual small talk or forming deep, meaningful connections, they find fulfillment in their relationships. Sanguines are typically excellent at building networks and friendships, thanks to their charm, humor, and ability to relate to people easily. However, because they seek social validation, they may sometimes overextend themselves or rely too heavily on others for emotional support.

## Strengths of the Sanguine Personality

- **Social Influence**: Sanguines have a natural ability to connect with people and make others feel at ease. This makes them great communicators, networkers, and often the glue that holds groups together. They can bring people from different walks of life together and make social interactions enjoyable.
- **Optimism and Positivity**: Their positive outlook on life can be a source of motivation for themselves and those around them. Sanguines are often the ones to inspire others to take risks or try new things, encouraging others to embrace opportunities with confidence.
- **Charisma**: Sanguines are often charismatic and can captivate audiences, whether in small group settings or larger social events. Their expressiveness, humor, and energy make them magnetic, and they tend to make lasting impressions on others.

## Challenges for the Sanguine Personality

- **Impulsiveness**: Their spontaneous nature can sometimes lead them to act without thinking things through, leading to poor decision-making or hasty actions. This impulsiveness can also cause them to overlook the consequences of their actions, especially in situations that require careful planning or consideration.
- **Disorganization**: Because sanguines enjoy variety and excitement, they may have difficulty sticking to routines or staying organized. They

might find it hard to prioritize tasks and can sometimes leave projects unfinished, focusing on the new and exciting rather than the mundane.

- **Superficiality**: Sanguines may sometimes struggle with depth in their relationships or interests, preferring to stay on the surface rather than delve into complex or serious matters. Their focus on fun and social interaction can sometimes make them appear superficial or inattentive to more meaningful aspects of life.

Sanguine individuals are often seen as the life of the party, capable of making any gathering feel vibrant and full of energy. Their ability to connect with others, their optimism, and their love for adventure make them beloved in many social circles. However, their need for novelty, impulsive nature, and tendency to avoid routine can also present challenges in their personal and professional lives. Understanding these traits can help sanguine individuals harness their strengths while addressing their areas for growth.

# Choleric: (The Natural Leader)

Choleric personalities are often described as natural-born leaders. They are assertive, driven, and highly motivated individuals who thrive in positions of authority and responsibility. People with a choleric personality are known for their ambition, decisiveness, and determination to achieve their goals. They are action-oriented and excel in environments where quick decision-making, efficiency, and results are key. Whether in the workplace, a social setting, or a crisis situation, choleric individuals are often the ones who take charge, rally others, and push forward to accomplish what needs to be done.

# Key Characteristics of Choleric Personality

1. **Ambitious and Goal-Oriented** Cholerics are incredibly driven by their desire to achieve success and make a lasting impact. Their ambitious nature pushes them to set high standards for themselves and those around them. They are constantly looking for opportunities to grow, advance, and achieve their goals. Whether in their career, personal life, or social endeavors, cholerics are focused on success and are always striving to reach the next milestone. Their goal-oriented mindset helps them stay motivated, even in the face of adversity.

2. **Decisive and Quick to Act** One of the most defining traits of a choleric personality is their decisiveness. Choleric individuals are not ones to linger over decisions or get bogged down by uncertainty. They make decisions quickly, often trusting their instincts and experience rather than overanalyzing situations. This decisiveness enables them to take action when others might hesitate. Whether it's making a business decision or choosing the best course of action in an emergency, cholerics are confident in their choices and quick to move forward.

3. **Assertive and Confident** Choleric people are assertive by nature. They have a strong presence and are not afraid to take charge in any situation. Their self-assurance often leads them to take leadership roles, whether formally or informally. They are clear about their needs, desires, and goals and are often vocal about them. This confidence allows them to express their opinions, set boundaries, and stand their ground when necessary. Cholerics rarely second-guess themselves, and their unwavering belief in their abilities can make them persuasive leaders.

4. **Independent and Self-Reliant** Choleric individuals value independence and are often self-sufficient. They prefer to rely on their own abilities and resources to achieve their objectives, rather than depending on others. This self-reliance gives them the strength to tackle challenges head-on and find solutions on their own. They are not afraid to take risks or go against the grain to achieve what they want. Because of their strong will and autonomy, cholerics are often seen as confident

and capable individuals who are comfortable making tough decisions without relying on external support.

5. **Pragmatic and Efficient** Cholerics are highly pragmatic and focused on results. They have little patience for inefficiency or wasted time. Their primary concern is achieving their goals, and they will seek out the most effective and efficient ways to get things done. Cholerics excel in environments where there is a need for practicality and action, as they can quickly assess a situation, make decisions, and move forward with a clear plan. Their emphasis on efficiency often makes them excellent problem-solvers who can cut through the complexities and find straightforward solutions.

6. **Strong-Willed and Determined** Choleric individuals are known for their strong will and determination. Once they set their mind to something, they are relentless in their pursuit of it. This persistence often enables them to overcome obstacles that would stop others in their tracks. Cholerics rarely give up, even in the face of adversity. Their determination to succeed can drive them to push through failures and setbacks, continuously striving for improvement and achievement.

7. **Authoritative and Commanding** Cholerics often take on leadership roles naturally because of their authoritative presence and commanding nature. They are comfortable being in charge and enjoy taking control of situations, especially when a clear direction is needed. Whether it's managing a team, overseeing a project, or making decisions for a group, cholerics are not afraid to assert their authority and guide others toward success. They tend to be respected (and sometimes feared) for their ability to lead with confidence and clarity.

8. **Impatient and Impulsive** While cholerics are driven by action, their quick decision-making and strong focus on results can also make them impatient. They tend to grow frustrated with delays, inefficiency, or those who are not as goal-oriented as they are. Cholerics may have little tolerance for what they perceive as indecision or lack of urgency. This impatience can sometimes lead to impulsiveness or rash decisions, especially when they feel pressured to act quickly. Their strong desire

to achieve can sometimes cause them to overlook important details or to push people too hard to meet their goals.

9. **Competitive and Achievement-Focused** Cholerics have a natural inclination toward competition. They thrive in competitive environments where they can measure their progress and achievements against others. This drive for success often pushes them to outdo themselves and others, seeking constant improvement. They enjoy challenges and are highly motivated by the prospect of winning or being the best at what they do. Cholerics tend to take great pride in their accomplishments, and their competitive nature often motivates them to push the boundaries of what they can achieve.

10. **Prone to Conflict and Dominance** Because of their strong personality and assertiveness, choleric individuals can sometimes come across as domineering or confrontational. They are not afraid to engage in conflict if it means asserting their point of view or securing their position. While they are generally willing to debate and argue their perspective, this trait can also make them appear overly aggressive or intolerant of opposing viewpoints. Their desire to control situations and lead can sometimes lead to clashes with others, especially those who are more passive or less decisive.

## Strengths of the Choleric Personality

- **Leadership and Initiative**: Cholerics excel in leadership roles due to their natural ability to take charge, make decisions quickly, and inspire others to take action. Their assertiveness and confidence make them effective leaders who can lead teams, organizations, or even social groups toward success.

- **Ambition and Determination**: The choleric personality is driven by a deep desire to succeed and accomplish their goals. This ambition is often the fuel behind their hard work and persistence. Their determination means they rarely give up, even in difficult situations.

- **Decisiveness and Action-Oriented**: Cholerics are quick decision-makers who are comfortable taking action. Their ability to make decisions under pressure and act without hesitation enables them to achieve their goals in a timely and efficient manner.

While the choleric personality has many strengths, it is essential to recognize that, like any personality type, there are challenges associated with this strong-willed nature. The key to personal growth for cholerics lies in learning to balance their assertiveness with patience and empathy, ensuring they can lead effectively without alienating others.

# Melancholic: (The Thoughtful Thinker)

The melancholic personality is often characterized by deep thinking, introspection, and a preference for order and structure. People with a melancholic temperament tend to be reflective, analytical, and sensitive. They are the "thoughtful thinkers" who meticulously analyze situations, consider the long-term impact of their actions, and pay attention to the finer details. While they may not always seek the spotlight, their intellectual depth and emotional richness make them valuable contributors to any setting. Melancholics are often the ones who offer thoughtful insights, solutions to problems, and a sense of calm when things are chaotic.

## Key Characteristics of Melancholic Personality

1. **Analytical and Detail-Oriented** One of the defining traits of a melancholic personality is their ability to think deeply and analyze situations from multiple angles. Melancholics tend to be highly logical and

observant, often noticing small details that others might overlook. They thrive in environments where critical thinking and careful consideration are needed. This ability to think through problems carefully allows them to come up with well-thought-out solutions, though it can sometimes lead to overthinking or indecisiveness when there is too much to process.

2. **Introverted and Reserved** Unlike their more extroverted counterparts, melancholics are typically introverted, preferring solitude or spending time in smaller, close-knit groups rather than large social gatherings. They value their alone time, during which they can reflect, read, write, or pursue their intellectual interests. Melancholics tend to be more reserved in their interactions and may feel drained by constant social interaction, especially with people they don't know well. They enjoy deep, meaningful conversations over superficial chit-chat and often form close, lasting friendships with a select few.

3. **Sensitive and Emotionally Deep** Melancholic individuals are known for their sensitivity, both emotionally and intellectually. They often have a rich inner life and are deeply moved by art, music, and literature. While they may not always express their emotions outwardly, they feel things very deeply. This emotional depth can make them empathetic and compassionate toward others, but it can also make them prone to sadness or melancholy, particularly if they are overwhelmed by life's challenges. Melancholics often find comfort in introspection, which helps them process their emotions and find clarity.

4. **Perfectionistic and High Standards** People with a melancholic personality often set very high standards for themselves and others. They strive for perfection in their work, relationships, and personal lives, which can drive them to excel in many areas. This perfectionism is rooted in their desire for things to be just right and their tendency to focus on the smallest details. While this trait can lead to outstanding achievements, it can also cause stress or frustration, especially when things don't go as planned or when their expectations are not met. Melancholics are often their own harshest critics, feeling dissatisfied with anything less than perfection.

5. **Organized and Structured** Melancholics thrive in environments where there is order and structure. They are typically highly organized individuals who take great care in planning and executing tasks. Whether it's managing their personal lives, work projects, or schedules, they value routine and predictability. They are meticulous planners who like to have everything mapped out in advance, and they often enjoy creating systems to ensure that tasks are completed efficiently and effectively. This love for structure can make them dependable and reliable, as they are unlikely to forget important details or commitments.

6. **Cautious and Thoughtful** Melancholic individuals tend to be cautious by nature. They think carefully before making decisions and weigh the pros and cons of every option. This careful consideration means that they are less likely to take risks impulsively or act without thoroughly analyzing the consequences. While this caution can help them avoid mistakes and setbacks, it can also lead to hesitation or missed opportunities. Melancholics may overanalyze situations, leading to indecision or a fear of making the wrong choice. However, their careful planning and consideration usually mean that they are well-prepared for any situation that comes their way.

7. **Loyal and Dependable** Although melancholics are often reserved and may take time to open up to others, they are fiercely loyal and dependable once they do. They tend to form deep, long-lasting bonds with those they trust and are committed to supporting their loved ones. In relationships, they are reliable and will often go to great lengths to ensure the happiness and well-being of their friends, family, and partners. Their loyalty is rooted in their emotional depth and their desire to nurture and care for those they hold dear. Once they feel a connection, they are unlikely to break it easily.

8. **Pessimistic and Prone to Worry** One of the challenges that melancholic individuals face is their tendency toward pessimism and worry. Because they tend to overthink situations and focus on potential problems, they can sometimes struggle with anxiety or negative thinking. They often anticipate the worst-case scenarios, which can lead to

feelings of doubt, insecurity, or fear. While they may be quick to identify potential issues, they can also be slow to see the positive aspects of a situation, leading to a more cynical or downbeat outlook. This pessimism can sometimes hold them back from pursuing new opportunities or taking risks, as they are preoccupied with potential failure.

9. **Introspective and Self-Aware** Melancholics spend a great deal of time reflecting on their thoughts, actions, and emotions. This introspection helps them develop a deep understanding of themselves and their motivations. They are often highly self-aware, constantly evaluating their strengths, weaknesses, and areas for improvement. While this self-awareness can lead to personal growth, it can also cause them to be overly critical of themselves. Melancholics may dwell on their mistakes or shortcomings, and this can sometimes hinder their progress or self-confidence. However, their introspective nature helps them learn from their experiences and make meaningful changes in their lives.

10. **Creative and Artistic** Despite their reserved and analytical nature, melancholics often possess a strong creative streak. Their emotional depth and sensitivity allow them to connect with art, music, and literature in a profound way. Many melancholic individuals have a talent for writing, painting, composing, or other forms of artistic expression. Their creativity is often fueled by their introspective thoughts and emotional experiences, and they may use artistic pursuits as a way to process their feelings or share their inner world with others. While they may not always seek recognition for their creativity, they often produce work that is thoughtful, meaningful, and impactful.

## Strengths of the Melancholic Personality

- **Deep Thinkers**: Melancholics have the ability to think critically and analyze situations with great depth. This makes them excellent problem-solvers and intellectuals, able to approach challenges from multiple angles and come up with well-reasoned solutions.

- **Organized and Reliable**: Their preference for structure and planning means that melancholics are often highly organized and dependable. They are meticulous in their work and personal lives, ensuring that tasks are completed to the highest standards.
- **Empathetic and Compassionate**: Melancholics are deeply sensitive to the emotions of others and are often highly empathetic. Their ability to understand and relate to the struggles of those around them makes them compassionate friends, family members, and colleagues.
- **Creative and Artistic**: Their emotional depth and introspective nature often lead to a strong creative drive. Melancholics are often talented in the arts, producing works that are thoughtful, poignant, and reflective of their inner world.

# Phlegmatic: The Peaceful Mediator

The phlegmatic personality is often described as calm, patient, and easygoing. People with a phlegmatic temperament are known for their peace-loving nature, and they tend to avoid conflict and confrontation whenever possible. Rather than seeking attention or dominance, phlegmatics value tranquility, stability, and harmonious relationships. They are naturally drawn to creating balance in their environment and are excellent at mediating disputes and bringing people together. In many ways, the phlegmatic individual is the "peacemaker," often serving as the glue that holds a group together and helps restore calm in tense situations.

# Key Characteristics of Phlegmatic Personality

1. **Calm and Relaxed** Phlegmatic individuals are often the calmest in any group setting. They are known for their ability to remain composed, even in stressful or chaotic situations. While others might become anxious or upset, phlegmatics tend to maintain a steady, unruffled demeanor. This ability to stay calm under pressure makes them excellent problem-solvers, as they are not easily overwhelmed by external factors. Their relaxed nature also makes them approachable and comforting to others who may be feeling stressed or tense.

2. **Patient and Tolerant** Patience is a hallmark of the phlegmatic personality. These individuals are tolerant of differences in others and are willing to give people the time and space they need. They don't rush through tasks or interactions and are typically very understanding when it comes to other people's emotions or behaviors. Phlegmatics are generally non-judgmental and open-minded, making them great listeners and companions for those who need to vent or express themselves.

3. **Easygoing and Low-Key** Phlegmatics are often described as "easygoing" because they don't let small annoyances or disruptions bother them. They tend to take life as it comes, adapting to situations with minimal resistance. This laid-back attitude allows them to be highly flexible and adaptable, as they are not easily thrown off course by unexpected events or changes. Phlegmatics are typically content with a quiet, simple lifestyle and are not driven by the desire for excitement or drama.

4. **Conflict-Avoidant** One of the defining characteristics of a phlegmatic personality is a strong aversion to conflict. These individuals do not like confrontation and will go out of their way to avoid arguments or emotional clashes. They tend to prefer peaceful resolutions and are often willing to compromise to keep the peace. While this conflict-avoidance can be beneficial in maintaining harmony, it can sometimes lead to issues being swept under the rug or not addressed directly. Phlegmatics might avoid difficult conversations, choosing instead to let things go rather than face uncomfortable situations.

5. **Empathetic and Compassionate** Phlegmatics are highly empathetic and compassionate individuals who are genuinely concerned about the well-being of others. They are often sensitive to the emotions and needs of those around them and are quick to offer comfort and support. Their caring nature makes them excellent friends, family members, and colleagues, as they tend to prioritize the happiness and needs of others. This empathy also enables them to understand different perspectives, making them effective mediators in times of disagreement or tension.

6. **Supportive and Loyal** Phlegmatics are incredibly supportive and loyal to their loved ones. They may not always be the most vocal in expressing their feelings, but their actions speak volumes. They are dependable and reliable friends who can always be counted on in times of need. Phlegmatics are dedicated to their relationships and are willing to make sacrifices to help others or maintain peace. Their loyalty and dedication make them the kind of person others can rely on when things get tough.

7. **Non-Competitive and Unambitious** Unlike choleric or sanguine personalities, phlegmatics are not driven by competition or the need to outperform others. They tend to be more focused on maintaining stability and enjoying life rather than striving for status, recognition, or achievement. Phlegmatics are content with a quieter, less demanding lifestyle, and they do not seek the limelight or the accolades that come with being in the spotlight. They are more likely to find fulfillment in personal relationships, hobbies, or simple pleasures than in ambitious pursuits.

8. **Pragmatic and Practical** Phlegmatic individuals are highly practical and grounded in reality. They tend to avoid overly complex or abstract ideas and focus instead on what is tangible and achievable. This practicality makes them great at managing everyday tasks and handling responsibilities in a straightforward manner. They may not be the ones to come up with wild or creative ideas, but they excel in putting plans into action and ensuring that things run smoothly. Their ability to remain grounded and focused on the present moment helps them make sound decisions and handle challenges efficiently.

9. **Indecisive and Passive** One of the challenges that phlegmatics face is indecisiveness. Because they value harmony and avoid conflict, they can sometimes have trouble making firm decisions, especially if those decisions could potentially upset others or create tension. Phlegmatics may struggle with asserting themselves and might take longer to reach a conclusion, often deferring to others or avoiding choices altogether. This passivity can sometimes lead to missed opportunities or an inability to take action when necessary. However, once they make a decision, they tend to stick with it and follow through.

10. **Dependable and Consistent** Phlegmatics are dependable and consistent in their actions and behavior. They are reliable individuals who can be counted on to follow through with their commitments, whether at work, in relationships, or in other areas of life. They are often steady and predictable, making them dependable in any situation. Their consistency makes them valuable team members, friends, and family members, as others know they can trust the phlegmatic person to do what they say they will do.

11. **Reluctant to Change** While phlegmatic individuals are adaptable, they tend to be more resistant to change than other personality types. They prefer the comfort of the familiar and may feel anxious or uncomfortable when faced with sudden changes or new environments. This reluctance to change can make phlegmatics seem rigid or slow to embrace new ideas, but it also contributes to their ability to maintain stability and order in their lives. They are not easily swayed by trends or external pressures, and they prefer to stick with what they know works for them.

## Strengths of the Phlegmatic Personality

- **Peacekeeping**: Phlegmatics excel at defusing tense situations and finding common ground in conflicts. Their calming presence and diplomatic nature allow them to bring people together and restore harmony in difficult circumstances.

- **Empathy and Supportiveness**: Phlegmatics are compassionate listeners and nurturing friends. They are excellent at providing emotional support to others, and their non-judgmental nature makes them great confidants.

- **Stability**: Phlegmatics provide a sense of stability and consistency in their relationships and environments. Their steady, predictable nature ensures that things run smoothly and people can rely on them for support.
- **Practicality**: Phlegmatics' practical approach to life makes them good at handling everyday tasks efficiently. Their grounded nature helps them stay focused and make sound decisions based on what is achievable and realistic.

# Chapter 3: How Your Personality Affects Your Relationships

## Understanding the Dynamics Between Different Types

Understanding how different personality types interact is crucial for fostering harmonious relationships, whether in the workplace, at home, or in social settings. Each personality type—sanguine, choleric, melancholic, and phlegmatic—has its own strengths and weaknesses, and understanding these dynamics can help mitigate conflict, enhance communication, and create more productive and supportive environments.

## How Different Personality Types Influence Each Other

1. **Sanguine and Choleric: Energy Meets Action** The interaction between sanguine and choleric personalities is dynamic and often energizing. Sanguines, with their social and enthusiastic nature, bring a sense of fun and excitement to the relationship, while cholerics provide direction, leadership, and focus. Cholerics may appreciate the energy and spontaneity that sanguines bring to the table, while sanguines may find cholerics' assertiveness and drive motivating.

However, the dynamic can also lead to friction. Sanguines' carefree and impulsive tendencies can sometimes clash with cholerics' need for control and efficiency. Cholerics may view sanguines as disorganized or overly social, while sanguines may find cholerics too rigid or controlling. Successful interactions between these two types often require mutual respect: sanguines need to respect cholerics' need for structure, and cholerics need to appreciate the joy and creativity that sanguines bring to their projects or relationships.

**2.Sanguine and Melancholic: Fun and Reflection** The relationship between a sanguine and a melancholic can be complementary, but also challenging. Sanguines' upbeat, optimistic nature can help lift melancholics, who are more introspective and serious. The sanguine's enthusiasm may encourage the melancholic to step out of their comfort zone and embrace new experiences, while the melancholic's depth and careful planning can help the sanguine reflect more seriously on their actions.

On the downside, melancholics may feel overwhelmed by the sanguine's incessant need for attention and socializing, while sanguines may find melancholics overly serious or too focused on the negatives. Effective communication between these two types is essential. Sanguines must be sensitive to the melancholic's need for quiet time and deeper reflection, while melancholics should try to embrace the sanguine's light-heartedness and enthusiasm.

**3.Sanguine and Phlegmatic: Excitement and Stability** Sanguines and phlegmatics can complement each other well, as they balance each other's extremes. Sanguines' energy and extroversion often provide excitement and motivation, while phlegmatics' calm and composed demeanor can help temper the sometimes erratic behavior of sanguines. Phlegmatics, who tend to avoid conflict, are a good grounding force for sanguines who may be impulsive or distracted.

However, this relationship can sometimes become imbalanced. Sanguines might feel that phlegmatics are too passive or slow to take action, while phlegmatics may view sanguines as too frenetic or chaotic. For this pairing to work, the sanguine must respect the phlegmatic's need for peace and stability, while the phlegmatic should try to engage more actively in the relationship and show enthusiasm.

**4.Choleric and Melancholic: Drive Meets Depth** Cholerics and melancholics can create a powerful combination when they work together, particularly in goal-oriented environments. Cholerics, with their drive and leadership abilities, can inspire melancholics to push forward, while melancholics' careful planning and attention to detail can help cholerics avoid mistakes and achieve their goals with precision. Cholerics tend to focus on the "big picture," while melancholics excel in making sure every element is well thought out.

On the flip side, these two types may struggle with communication due to their differing approaches. Cholerics may perceive melancholics as overly cautious or pessimistic, while melancholics may find cholerics too aggressive or insensitive to their need for perfection and detail. The key to a successful interaction lies in mutual respect for each other's strengths. Cholerics need to appreciate the importance of careful planning and reflection, while melancholics should recognize the importance of decisive action and leadership.

**5.Choleric and Phlegmatic: Leadership and Calm** The combination of choleric and phlegmatic personalities can be quite effective, especially when the phlegmatic is in a supportive role to the choleric's leadership. Cholerics' decisive and goal-oriented nature is complemented by the phlegmatic's ability to remain calm and composed, especially during challenging situations. Phlegmatics often make great team members in a choleric-led environment, as they are reliable, patient, and diplomatic, which helps keep things running smoothly.

However, tension can arise if the choleric becomes frustrated with the phlegmatic's slower pace or apparent lack of initiative. Cholerics might see phlegmatics as passive or unmotivated, while phlegmatics may feel overwhelmed or bossed around by the choleric's assertive nature. For this pairing to work, the choleric must respect the phlegmatic's need for stability and avoid being overly domineering, while the phlegmatic should be more proactive and assertive in taking on responsibilities.

**6.Melancholic and Phlegmatic: Depth Meets Calm** The dynamic between melancholic and phlegmatic individuals is often one of mutual understanding and support. Both types value stability and are typically reserved, making it easier for them to connect on a deeper emotional level without the need for constant excitement or social interaction. Melancholics appreciate the phlegmatic's ability to remain calm and offer practical solutions during times of stress, while phlegmatics admire the melancholic's intellectual depth and thoughtful approach to life.

However, these two types may struggle with taking action when it is needed. Both tend to be cautious and may avoid confrontation or difficult decisions, leading to indecision or stagnation. Phlegmatics may rely too much on the melancholic's analysis, while melancholics may become frustrated by the phlegmatic's passive nature. To avoid stagnation, both need to encourage each other to step out of their comfort zones and take initiative when necessary.

**7.Choleric and Sanguine: Action and Enthusiasm** The relationship between choleric and sanguine personalities is often energetic and action-driven. Cholerics are goal-oriented and determined, while sanguines are enthusiastic and social. Together, they can accomplish great things, with the choleric pushing for results and the sanguine motivating others along the way. This combination can be highly effective in leadership roles, team settings, or situations that require quick decision-making and enthusiasm.

However, the high energy of the sanguine can sometimes clash with the choleric's need for control. Cholerics may view sanguines as disorganized or too distracted, while sanguines may feel constrained by the choleric's focus on efficiency. Both types need to respect each other's approach—cholerics must allow room for the creativity and energy of sanguines, while sanguines should acknowledge the importance of discipline and structure in the choleric's world.

# Conflict Resolution: How to Manage Personality Clashes

Conflict is an inevitable part of human interaction, especially when people with different personality types come together. Whether in personal relationships, workplaces, or social groups, understanding the causes of personality clashes and learning effective strategies to manage them is crucial. Each personality type—sanguine, choleric, melancholic, and phlegmatic—has its own unique strengths, challenges, and ways of responding to conflict. By recognizing these differences and applying appropriate conflict resolution strategies, it is possible to transform clashes into opportunities for growth, better understanding, and stronger relationships.

## Understanding the Roots of Personality Clashes

The first step in managing personality conflicts is to understand why clashes occur. Different personality types have different priorities, communication styles, and ways of approaching problems, which can lead to misunderstandings and frustration.

- **Sanguine personalities** are social, energetic, and spontaneous. They can come across as disorganized or overly talkative to more reserved or goal-focused types like melancholics or cholerics.
- **Choleric personalities** are driven, assertive, and goal-oriented, often preferring quick action and efficiency. This can clash with the more laid-back, thoughtful nature of phlegmatics or the careful, detail-oriented approach of melancholics.
- **Melancholic personalities** tend to be deep thinkers who value structure, order, and careful planning. They may feel overwhelmed or frustrated by the more spontaneous or chaotic nature of sanguines or the fast-paced decision-making of cholerics.
- **Phlegmatic personalities** are calm, patient, and conflict-averse. They might struggle with the assertiveness or decisiveness of cholerics and

can feel frustrated by the lack of energy or urgency in melancholics and sanguines.

## Strategies for Managing Personality Clashes

1. **Practice Active Listening** The foundation of any conflict resolution strategy is effective communication, and this begins with active listening. Each personality type tends to focus on different things in a conversation, and miscommunication often arises when people do not listen fully to each other's concerns or needs.

- **Sanguine individuals** might interrupt or speak over others out of excitement or to keep the conversation lively. In these situations, the other party might feel unheard or dismissed.
- **Cholerics** might dominate the conversation or make decisions too quickly, leaving little room for others to express their perspectives.
- **Melancholics** may hold back their opinions or feelings, especially if they think others are not taking the conversation seriously enough.
- **Phlegmatics** might withdraw or avoid confrontation altogether, leaving their true feelings unspoken.

To resolve conflicts, all parties need to practice active listening—meaning truly focusing on the speaker, asking clarifying questions, and reflecting back what has been said to ensure understanding. This helps to acknowledge each person's perspective and fosters empathy.

**2.Acknowledge and Respect Differences** Each personality type has its own way of processing information, making decisions, and approaching life. Acknowledging and respecting these differences is essential to conflict resolution. It is important to recognize that personality clashes are often rooted in differences in values, priorities, or communication styles, rather than in malicious intent.

- **Cholerics** should recognize that not everyone is comfortable with fast decision-making or pressure. Allowing space for others to contribute can lead to more balanced and thoughtful decisions.
- **Melancholics** need to understand that not everyone requires the same level of detail or careful planning. Sometimes, a more flexible and quick approach is necessary.
- **Sanguines** should be aware of how their spontaneous nature can overwhelm others who prefer routine or predictability. They can help by allowing others the time to process and respond.
- **Phlegmatics** must understand that sometimes being too passive can cause frustration in more assertive types who need direction or a sense of urgency.

By recognizing and valuing each other's differences, it becomes easier to find common ground and address conflict in a respectful way.

**3.Stay Calm and Manage Emotions** In any conflict, emotions can run high. However, keeping emotions in check is key to resolving the situation effectively. This is particularly important for those who are naturally more reactive—like cholerics—who may become frustrated quickly, or melancholics, who might internalize feelings and withdraw.

- **Sanguine personalities** tend to be more emotional and may react impulsively, which can escalate tensions. They should try to take a moment to pause and think before speaking or acting.
- **Cholerics** can sometimes be quick to anger, especially if they feel their authority or leadership is being challenged. Taking deep breaths or stepping away from the situation momentarily can help them regain composure.
- **Melancholics** may retreat into their thoughts or become overly critical, so it is essential for them to communicate their feelings without suppressing them or getting lost in analysis.
- **Phlegmatics** are generally calm, but they may also be passive-aggressive if they feel overwhelmed or unappreciated. It's important for them to

express their opinions clearly, rather than letting frustration build.

When emotions are managed, conversations tend to be more productive, and solutions are more likely to be reached.

**4.Compromise and Find Common Ground** Compromise is often necessary to resolve conflicts, particularly when the parties involved have conflicting needs or priorities. Finding common ground helps each individual feel heard and valued, and it leads to a solution that meets everyone's basic needs.

- **Sanguine and phlegmatic personalities** may need to meet halfway on social activities, with the sanguine taking the lead on planning events while allowing space for the phlegmatic to choose quieter, more low-key options.
- **Cholerics and melancholics** may need to find a balance between speed and thoroughness. Cholerics should respect the melancholic's need for preparation, while melancholics can be more flexible in their timelines to accommodate the choleric's need for swift action.

Encouraging compromise shows that each party is willing to give and take, which helps build trust and strengthen relationships.

**5.Set Boundaries and Be Direct** In some situations, clear boundaries and direct communication are essential for conflict resolution. For example, if someone feels overwhelmed by another person's actions or behavior, it's important to express those feelings in a calm, respectful way without being passive-aggressive or hostile.

- **Choleric individuals** may need to be mindful of how their assertiveness affects others, especially when working with more passive personality types like phlegmatics.
- **Phlegmatic personalities** should be encouraged to express their feelings

and concerns more openly, rather than avoiding difficult conversations or being too passive.

- **Sanguines** may need to be reminded that their tendency to dominate a conversation can leave others feeling unheard, requiring them to be more mindful of taking turns to listen and respond.
- **Melancholics** can benefit from setting clear expectations for themselves and others, and being open to receiving direct feedback, which will help prevent misunderstandings.

By setting boundaries and communicating directly, conflicts can be addressed before they escalate into bigger issues.

# Strengthening Personal and Professional Relationships

Building and maintaining strong personal and professional relationships is essential for happiness, productivity, and success. Whether it's with family, friends, colleagues, or clients, healthy relationships are based on mutual respect, trust, effective communication, and understanding. By strengthening relationships, we improve not only our social bonds but also our overall well-being. Each personality type brings unique strengths and challenges to relationships, and understanding these dynamics can significantly improve how we connect with others.

## 1. Understanding and Embracing Personality Differences

One of the most fundamental steps in strengthening relationships is understanding that people have different personality traits, temperaments, and preferences. When we appreciate these differences, we are better equipped to navigate conflicts and foster harmonious interactions.

- **Sanguine individuals** bring energy, enthusiasm, and creativity to relationships. They are often the life of the party and can inspire others to be more social and adventurous. However, they may need help maintaining focus or respecting others' need for quiet time. By acknowledging that they thrive in lively environments and enjoy spontaneous experiences, others can learn to appreciate their zest for life while encouraging them to be more mindful of others' boundaries.
- **Choleric personalities** offer leadership, decisiveness, and ambition. They can drive projects forward and motivate others. However, their assertiveness can sometimes come off as domineering or impatient. Cholerics benefit from recognizing the need for collaboration, showing appreciation for others' contributions, and being open to feedback. In relationships, understanding that not everyone shares their urgency can help create more balanced dynamics.
- **Melancholic individuals** are known for their thoughtfulness, attention to detail, and deep emotional understanding. Their reflective nature can bring depth to relationships, but their tendency toward perfectionism and sensitivity to criticism may lead to misunderstandings. By practicing self-compassion and being more flexible, melancholics can connect with others on a more relaxed and approachable level.
- **Phlegmatic personalities** offer calm, patience, and stability. They are often reliable and supportive, providing a sense of peace in chaotic situations. However, their tendency to avoid confrontation and take a passive approach can sometimes make it difficult to address problems head-on. Phlegmatics can strengthen relationships by being more proactive in expressing their needs and participating more actively in decision-making.

## 2. Communication: The Cornerstone of Connection

Effective communication is at the heart of all strong relationships. Clear, open, and honest communication builds trust and helps resolve conflicts before they escalate. Each personality type communicates differently, and understanding these differences can improve how we convey and receive messages.

- **Sanguines** are talkative and enthusiastic communicators. They enjoy engaging others in conversation and tend to share personal stories and experiences. However, they may interrupt or become distracted, especially in group settings. To strengthen communication with sanguines, it's important to be patient, allow them to express themselves fully, and gently bring them back to the topic at hand if they wander.
- **Cholerics** are direct and assertive. They appreciate clear and concise communication and may become frustrated if conversations feel unproductive or overly vague. When communicating with cholerics, it's essential to be clear, organized, and respectful of their time. They appreciate goal-oriented discussions and value people who are confident in their ideas.
- **Melancholics** are more reserved and thoughtful in their communication. They may take time to process information before responding and often prefer deeper, more meaningful conversations. To connect with melancholics, it's important to create a safe space for them to share their thoughts and emotions. Listening actively and asking reflective questions can help them open up.
- **Phlegmatics** are calm and diplomatic in their communication. They prefer to listen more than speak and often avoid confrontation. When speaking with phlegmatics, it's important to be patient and not push them to make quick decisions. Encouraging them to express their opinions in a supportive environment helps them feel more comfortable and confident in sharing their thoughts.

## 3. Conflict Resolution and Managing Disagreements

Disagreements are inevitable in any relationship, but how we handle conflict can determine the strength of that relationship. Each personality type approaches conflict differently, and understanding these tendencies can help reduce tension and foster resolution.

- **Sanguines** can be overly emotional or impulsive during conflicts, and may seek to resolve issues quickly by talking through them. They may be more likely to avoid serious confrontations or try to defuse the situation with humor. To resolve conflicts with sanguines, it's important to stay calm and give them space to express their feelings, while also encouraging them to stay focused on finding a solution rather than just smoothing things over.

- **Cholerics** are natural problem-solvers but can become confrontational or overly dominant when they feel their authority or ideas are challenged. They may push for quick resolutions and dismiss slower, more collaborative approaches. When resolving conflict with cholerics, it's crucial to remain calm, assertive, and solution-focused, providing clear arguments to support your point of view while respecting their leadership.

- **Melancholics** tend to internalize conflict and may become withdrawn or overly critical of themselves or others. They are often sensitive to perceived slights and may struggle to forgive or forget easily. To resolve conflicts with melancholics, it's important to approach the situation with empathy and understanding, acknowledging their feelings and giving them time to process before expecting resolution.

- **Phlegmatics** typically avoid conflict and may struggle to express their true feelings during disagreements. They may agree to avoid confrontation or delay addressing issues, leading to passive-aggressive behavior. To resolve conflicts with phlegmatics, it's important to encourage open dialogue, gently prompting them to express their thoughts and concerns. Providing a non-judgmental and supportive space helps them feel safe in voicing their feelings.

## 4. Building Trust and Respect

Trust is the foundation of any successful relationship. For relationships to flourish, both parties need to feel secure and valued. Each personality type may require different approaches to build and maintain trust.

- **Sanguines** value appreciation and attention. They thrive when they feel recognized and validated for their contributions, especially in social settings. To build trust with sanguines, regularly acknowledge their efforts and maintain open communication, particularly when they are feeling overlooked.
- **Cholerics** value competence and reliability. They trust individuals who can make decisions quickly and act decisively. To gain their trust, it's essential to demonstrate your ability to take initiative, stay organized, and follow through on commitments.
- **Melancholics** value loyalty and honesty. They may be more reserved and cautious in trusting others, but once trust is built, they are deeply loyal. To build trust with melancholics, show consistency in your actions, be transparent, and avoid making promises you can't keep.
- **Phlegmatics** value stability and emotional security. They trust individuals who are patient, reliable, and non-judgmental. To build trust with phlegmatics, show them that you can be counted on, remain steady in your interactions, and offer support when needed without rushing them to make decisions.

## 5. Encouraging Growth and Mutual Support

In both personal and professional relationships, it's important to encourage growth and mutual support. By supporting each other's goals, ambitions, and personal development, relationships become more rewarding and meaningful. Each personality type brings unique strengths that can contribute to the growth of the relationship.

- **Sanguines** can help others embrace new experiences and bring a sense of joy and adventure to the relationship. They encourage spontaneity and creativity, making them great partners for those seeking new opportunities.
- **Cholerics** can drive others toward achievement, motivating them to take charge of their goals and ambitions. They provide direction and vision, helping those around them stay focused on the bigger picture.
- **Melancholics** contribute depth, introspection, and problem-solving skills to relationships. Their ability to think critically and reflect on experiences can lead to personal growth and help others gain valuable insights.
- **Phlegmatics** offer patience, emotional stability, and quiet strength. They provide a steady, calming influence and support others in maintaining balance and harmony during times of change or stress.

By leveraging each personality type's strengths, individuals can encourage and support each other's personal and professional growth, leading to more fulfilling and lasting relationships.

# Chapter 4: The Impact of Childhood on Behavior

**T**he First Years: Shaping Your Future Personality
The early years of life are incredibly influential in shaping our personality. The experiences, interactions, and environments we encounter during this period play a key role in defining who we become as individuals. While personality is often thought to be largely innate or determined by genetics, the first few years of life lay a foundational blueprint that is heavily influenced by the way we are raised, our early relationships, and the social and cultural contexts we are part of. Understanding how personality develops during these formative years can provide insights into how we grow, adapt, and interact with others throughout our lives.

## 1. The Role of Genetics and Temperament

From birth, a child's temperament—their inherent behavioral tendencies—plays a significant role in shaping their personality. Research suggests that some aspects of our personality, such as our level of activity, sociability, and emotional reactivity, are influenced by our genetic makeup. These traits tend to be visible even in infancy.

- **Inborn Traits**: Some children are naturally more easygoing and content, while others may be more intense, sensitive, or fussy. For example, some babies are naturally calm and easy to soothe, while others may be more irritable or difficult to comfort. These early temperamental traits can provide the first clues to their future personality, whether they develop into sociable sanguines, determined cholerics, thoughtful melancholics, or calm phlegmatics.

- **The Influence of Early Bonding**: The early attachment between a child and their primary caregivers, typically parents, can greatly affect how children develop emotionally and socially. Secure attachments—where a child feels safe, nurtured, and understood—can lay the groundwork for a confident, resilient personality. On the other hand, insecure attachment, such as neglect or inconsistent caregiving, can lead to difficulties with trust, emotional regulation, and relationship-building later in life.

## 2. The Influence of Parenting Styles

Parenting plays a critical role in shaping a child's personality in the first few years. The way parents interact with their child, set boundaries, provide nurturing, and offer guidance can influence the development of key personality traits. There are several different parenting styles, each contributing to personality development in unique ways.

- **Authoritative Parenting**: This style, characterized by warmth, responsiveness, and clear expectations, is often associated with the most balanced and well-adjusted personalities. Children raised by authoritative parents tend to develop self-confidence, independence, and social competence. They also learn how to handle conflict constructively, which helps them navigate relationships as they grow older.

- **Authoritarian Parenting**: This style is strict and often involves high expectations with little room for flexibility or emotional expression. While children raised in such environments may develop strong self-discipline, they might also struggle with social skills, assertiveness, and creativity. These children may be more prone to anxiety, perfectionism, or issues with authority.

- **Permissive Parenting**: Permissive parents tend to be lenient, indulgent, and less likely to impose strict rules or boundaries. While children raised in this environment may feel loved and free to express themselves, they may also lack the structure needed to develop responsibility, impulse control, or resilience. This can lead to difficulties in handling challenges as they get older.

- **Neglectful Parenting**: Children raised in an environment where their basic needs for attention, care, or emotional support are not consistently met may develop attachment issues, low self-esteem, and difficulties with trust and intimacy. This can lead to problems with emotional regulation, social interactions, and future relationships.

## 3. Social and Environmental Factors

Beyond the immediate family environment, the broader social and environmental influences during the first years of life also play a significant role in shaping personality. The interactions a child has with peers, caregivers, and even the community can affect how they see themselves and others.

- **Early Socialization**: In the early years, children begin to learn the social norms, values, and behaviors that guide their interactions with others. Positive early social experiences, like making friends, sharing, and learning empathy, can help foster emotional intelligence and positive relationship-building skills. For example, a child who is encouraged to share and interact with other children may develop into a sociable and empathetic adult.
- **Cultural Influence**: The culture a child is raised in can also have a profound impact on personality development. For instance, in collectivist cultures, where the focus is often on community and family, children may develop a strong sense of interdependence and responsibility to others. In contrast, individualistic cultures may encourage more independent, self-reliant personalities.
- **Early Education and Learning**: The types of learning experiences a child has in the early years—whether at home, in daycare, or in

preschool—also influence personality development. A stimulating environment that encourages curiosity, exploration, and creativity can foster a child's cognitive and emotional growth. In contrast, an environment lacking in stimulation or one that discourages exploration may hinder development in these areas.

## 4. Emotional and Social Development

Emotions and social skills develop rapidly during the first years of life. The way a child learns to express, manage, and understand their emotions has a lasting effect on their personality.

- **Emotional Regulation**: In the early years, children begin to learn how to regulate their emotions with the help of their caregivers. Secure and consistent emotional support helps children develop the ability to cope with frustration, disappointment, and other emotions in healthy ways. Those who experience a lack of emotional support may have difficulty managing stress or regulating their emotions as they grow older.
- **Social Competence**: The way children interact with others during their early years—through play, shared activities, or problem-solving—helps them develop key social skills. These skills form the foundation for how a child will interact with peers, teachers, and adults in the future. Children who receive positive reinforcement for social interactions and cooperation may grow up to be more socially confident and empathetic.

## 5. The Role of Early Experiences in Shaping Personality Traits

The experiences children have in their early years can strongly influence the development of specific personality traits. For example, children who experience a lot of success and praise during their formative years may develop high self-esteem and confidence, leading to a choleric personality type. Those who are given the space and support to explore their feelings and the world around them may develop a more thoughtful, reflective melancholic personality. Similarly, children who grow up in supportive, stable environments may develop a phlegmatic temperament, valuing calm and peace in their adult relationships.

# Parental Influence and Early Experiences

The influence of parents and caregivers during a child's early years is one of the most powerful forces in shaping personality. From infancy through early childhood, the way children are nurtured, guided, and supported directly impacts their emotional development, social skills, and the way they perceive the world. The early experiences that children have within their family environment lay the foundation for how they will later interact with others, handle stress, and form relationships. Understanding the role of parental influence and early experiences helps explain why each person is unique in their approach to life, and how these early interactions can contribute to both strengths and challenges in adulthood.

## 1. Attachment and Emotional Security

One of the most significant contributions parents make to their child's personality development is through the establishment of a secure emotional bond, known as attachment. Attachment theory, developed by psychologist John Bowlby, suggests that the quality of the early bond between a child and their caregiver(s) affects the child's emotional well-being and ability to form relationships later in life.

- **Secure Attachment**: When a child feels consistently loved, protected, and safe, they develop secure attachment. This sense of security helps children explore the world with confidence and builds a solid foundation for emotional regulation, trust, and social competence. Children with secure attachment tend to be more resilient, exhibit higher levels of empathy, and form healthier, more trusting relationships as adults. They are more likely to approach new situations and challenges with curiosity and confidence.

- **Insecure Attachment**: Conversely, if a child's early emotional needs are not consistently met, they may develop insecure attachment styles. These include anxious attachment, where a child feels uncertain about whether their needs will be met, and avoidant attachment, where a child learns to suppress their emotional needs because they feel that no one will respond. Children with insecure attachment may struggle with anxiety, relationship difficulties, and low self-esteem later in life. They may also have trouble trusting others or managing their emotions in stressful situations.

## 2. Parenting Styles and Their Impact

The way parents raise their children—what rules, expectations, and emotional responses they provide—also plays a significant role in shaping a child's personality. Psychologist Diana Baumrind identified four primary parenting styles: authoritative, authoritarian, permissive, and neglectful. These styles influence children's behavior, attitudes, and future emotional health.

- **Authoritative Parenting**: This style is characterized by a balance of warmth and discipline. Authoritative parents are responsive to their children's needs and emotions, set clear expectations, and encourage independence while maintaining limits. Children raised by authoritative parents tend to develop high self-esteem, self-control, and social competence. They are often confident, able to express themselves clearly, and tend to have healthy relationships with others. This parenting style supports the development of a well-rounded and resilient personality.
- **Authoritarian Parenting**: Authoritarian parents are strict, often using

control and discipline to manage behavior, with little room for flexibility or emotional support. While this approach may produce children who are obedient and well-behaved in the short term, it can have negative consequences in the long run. Children raised by authoritarian parents may develop lower self-esteem, be more prone to anxiety, and have difficulty with decision-making or assertiveness. These children may also struggle to express their emotions openly and may be more likely to internalize their feelings of frustration.

- **Permissive Parenting**: Permissive parents are indulgent and lenient, placing few demands on their children. These parents tend to be nurturing and responsive but struggle to set clear boundaries. While permissive parenting can create a loving and warm environment, children raised in this way may lack the structure and discipline needed to develop responsibility, independence, and respect for authority. These children might also struggle with impulse control and may find it difficult to handle frustration or disappointment.

- **Neglectful Parenting**: Neglectful parenting, marked by a lack of emotional support, attention, and guidance, can lead to significant emotional and behavioral issues. Children raised by neglectful parents may struggle with low self-worth, attachment issues, and difficulties in forming healthy relationships. These children may develop a sense of insecurity, leading them to feel unworthy of love or care. In extreme cases, neglectful parenting can contribute to more serious behavioral issues, such as difficulty with impulse control, social withdrawal, or aggression.

## 3. The Influence of Early Experiences on Personality Traits

In addition to parenting styles, the specific experiences a child has during their formative years can significantly influence the development of their personality. Early childhood experiences can either reinforce or challenge a child's natural temperament, emotional responses, and social interactions.

- **Experiences of Success or Failure**: Early successes, such as achieving a milestone or receiving praise for a job well done, can help build a child's confidence and self-esteem. On the other hand, repeated failures or criticism without constructive feedback may lead to feelings of inadequacy or self-doubt. The way children are supported through both their successes and failures shapes their beliefs about their abilities, which in turn impacts their overall personality and approach to challenges.

- **Socialization and Peer Relationships**: A child's early social interactions with peers, siblings, and extended family also contribute to their personality development. Positive social experiences can help children develop essential social skills such as empathy, sharing, and cooperation, which are foundational for building healthy relationships later in life. Conversely, negative social experiences, such as bullying or isolation, can contribute to feelings of insecurity, mistrust, or social withdrawal.

- **Exposure to Stress or Trauma**: Early exposure to stress, trauma, or hardship—such as parental conflict, financial instability, illness, or abuse—can have profound effects on personality development. Chronic stress in early childhood can lead to difficulties in emotional regulation, increased anxiety, and a heightened tendency toward emotional reactivity. In extreme cases, unresolved trauma can contribute to personality disorders or other mental health issues.

- **Cultural and Environmental Factors**: The broader environment in which a child is raised also influences their personality development. Cultural values, societal expectations, and the availability of resources all play a role in shaping how children interact with the world. For instance, children raised in environments that emphasize collective well-being and community may develop stronger interpersonal skills, while those in more individualistic cultures may focus more on personal achievement and independence.

# 4. The Role of Early Education and Caregiving

The experiences children have outside of the home, particularly during their early education, also play a role in personality development. High-quality early education programs and positive caregiving relationships can have a lasting impact on a child's emotional and cognitive growth.

- **Preschool and Early Learning**: Early childhood education programs provide children with their first formal exposure to group learning, teamwork, and structured environments. Positive early education experiences help children develop cognitive skills, emotional regulation, and social competence. Children who are encouraged to ask questions, explore their environment, and engage with peers are more likely to develop a love for learning and an adaptable personality.
- **Caregivers and Teachers as Role Models**: The adults who care for and teach children outside the family also influence their emotional development. Supportive and nurturing caregivers help children develop positive social and emotional skills, such as resilience, self-control, and empathy. Conversely, caregivers who are inconsistent, uninvolved, or punitive may contribute to emotional difficulties or behavioral challenges.

Early life experiences, particularly those influenced by parental interactions and caregiving, play a central role in shaping personality. The emotional security a child feels, the type of parenting they receive, the challenges they encounter, and the broader cultural and social environment all leave lasting imprints that affect how they view themselves and others as they grow. Understanding these early influences helps explain the nuances of personality development and how we carry these traits into adulthood.

# Overcoming Childhood Challenges in Adulthood

Many aspects of our childhood—whether related to family dynamics, social experiences, or individual struggles—can leave lasting imprints on our personality and emotional well-being as adults. These early challenges may shape how we view ourselves, relate to others, and respond to stress or adversity. However, it's possible to overcome the challenges of childhood in adulthood through self-awareness, personal growth, and the development of coping strategies. Understanding the impact of childhood difficulties and how they can be addressed in adulthood is crucial for healing and creating a fulfilling life.

## 1. Acknowledging and Understanding Childhood Struggles

The first step in overcoming childhood challenges is acknowledging their impact. Whether it's a traumatic event, neglect, inconsistent parenting, or emotional wounds, recognizing that these experiences have shaped your beliefs, behaviors, and emotional responses is crucial. Understanding the root of certain adult patterns—such as a fear of abandonment, difficulty trusting others, or struggles with self-esteem—can help make sense of the behaviors and reactions that often seem confusing or unexplainable.

- **Trauma and Neglect**: For many individuals, childhood trauma, such as emotional or physical abuse, neglect, or loss, can leave deep scars. These early experiences may result in chronic feelings of insecurity, difficulty forming close relationships, or emotional numbness. The impact of trauma can also lead to anxiety, depression, or low self-worth in adulthood. Identifying the effects of trauma allows individuals to begin the process of healing.
- **Inconsistent Parenting**: Growing up in an environment with inconsistent or unpredictable caregiving, such as overly permissive or authoritarian parenting styles, can lead to confusion about boundaries and a lack of emotional regulation. These early experiences can manifest

in adulthood as difficulties with decision-making, authority issues, or struggles with emotional expression.

- **Social Challenges**: Bullying, social isolation, or difficulties with peer relationships during childhood can have long-lasting effects on self-confidence and social anxiety in adulthood. People who faced exclusion or were made to feel different in their formative years may struggle to connect with others later in life or have a heightened fear of rejection.

## 2. Building Self-Awareness and Emotional Intelligence

One of the most powerful tools for overcoming childhood challenges in adulthood is building self-awareness. Understanding how past experiences influence current emotions, behaviors, and relationships allows individuals to break free from patterns that no longer serve them. Self-awareness can be developed through reflection, mindfulness, and emotional intelligence.

- **Mindfulness and Reflection**: Mindfulness techniques—such as meditation, journaling, or simply taking time to pause and reflect—can help individuals become more in tune with their emotions. This process allows them to notice when old patterns or triggers from childhood arise and choose healthier ways of responding. Reflection on childhood experiences, perhaps with the help of therapy, can help uncover the root causes of adult struggles.
- **Emotional Intelligence (EQ)**: Emotional intelligence is the ability to recognize, understand, and manage our emotions, as well as to empathize with others. Developing EQ can be especially helpful for individuals who faced emotional neglect or rejection in childhood. By learning how to better regulate emotions, communicate effectively, and understand others' emotional cues, adults can form stronger, more supportive relationships and improve their overall emotional health.

## 3. Rewriting Limiting Beliefs

Childhood challenges often lead to the formation of limiting beliefs—deeply ingrained thoughts or assumptions about oneself and the world. For example, someone who experienced rejection in childhood might believe, "I am unworthy of love," or "People will always leave me." These beliefs can limit growth and contribute to behaviors that reinforce feelings of inadequacy or fear.

- **Identifying Limiting Beliefs**: The first step in rewriting limiting beliefs is identifying them. Reflecting on childhood messages—whether from parents, peers, or society—that may have contributed to these beliefs is essential. Once these beliefs are recognized, individuals can begin to challenge them by examining the evidence that supports or contradicts them.
- **Cognitive Behavioral Techniques**: Cognitive Behavioral Therapy (CBT) offers effective strategies for challenging and reframing negative beliefs. By recognizing distorted thinking patterns (such as catastrophizing or black-and-white thinking), individuals can begin to replace limiting beliefs with more positive and empowering ones. For example, someone who feels unworthy of success can start to focus on their achievements and the evidence that they are capable and deserving.

## 4. Healing Emotional Wounds Through Therapy

Therapy is a valuable tool for overcoming childhood challenges. Whether through individual therapy, group therapy, or trauma-informed care, therapy can provide a safe space to process and heal past wounds. Working with a trained therapist allows individuals to gain insight into their emotional struggles, develop coping mechanisms, and address unresolved childhood issues.

- **Talk Therapy**: Traditional talk therapy allows individuals to express and explore painful emotions related to childhood experiences. By articulating feelings, individuals gain a better understanding of how these experiences have shaped their adult behavior and mindset. Therapy also offers tools for managing these emotions more effectively.

- **Trauma-Informed Therapy**: For those who have experienced significant trauma in childhood, trauma-informed therapy can be especially helpful. Approaches such as Eye Movement Desensitization and Reprocessing (EMDR) or somatic therapies focus on processing the emotional and physical effects of trauma. These methods can help release stored emotions, reduce trauma-related symptoms, and promote healing.

- **Support Groups**: Support groups provide a space where individuals can connect with others who have had similar experiences. Sharing stories, offering mutual support, and learning coping strategies from others can be an empowering way to heal. Support groups can be particularly valuable for individuals who have faced specific challenges, such as childhood abuse or neglect.

## 5. Developing New Coping Strategies

As adults, we often face situations that trigger old childhood patterns, such as stress, conflict, or feelings of insecurity. Developing healthy coping strategies is essential for managing these triggers and reducing their negative impact on our lives. Instead of relying on maladaptive behaviors like avoidance or substance use, individuals can learn healthier ways of coping.

- **Healthy Stress Management**: Learning to manage stress in healthy ways can help individuals avoid repeating unhealthy patterns from childhood. Techniques such as exercise, deep breathing, progressive muscle relaxation, and yoga can help reduce stress and promote emotional resilience.

- **Building Strong Support Networks**: Having a network of friends, family, or colleagues who provide support, understanding, and validation can be essential for overcoming childhood challenges. Positive, stable relationships help individuals build trust, gain confidence, and navigate difficult situations more effectively.

- **Self-Care and Boundaries**: Setting healthy boundaries and prioritizing self-care is crucial for emotional well-being. Many adults who faced challenges in childhood may have learned to neglect their own needs or boundaries. By establishing clear boundaries and practicing self-compassion, individuals can cultivate a healthier, more balanced approach to relationships and personal growth.

## 6. Rebuilding Trust and Relationships

For adults who struggled with trust and attachment issues due to childhood experiences, rebuilding trust in relationships can be a significant challenge. However, it is possible to develop deeper, more secure relationships by working through past pain and being patient with the process.

- **Building Trust Gradually**: Rebuilding trust in relationships—whether with romantic partners, family, or friends—takes time and requires consistent effort. By setting clear expectations, communicating openly, and showing vulnerability, individuals can begin to build trust gradually. It's essential to be patient and gentle with oneself during this process.
- **Forgiveness and Letting Go**: For some individuals, overcoming childhood challenges involves forgiving those who may have caused emotional harm. Forgiveness doesn't necessarily mean excusing past actions, but rather releasing the emotional hold that those experiences have on your present. This can be a powerful step in healing and moving forward.

By addressing the emotional and psychological scars left by childhood challenges, adults can break free from limiting patterns, heal wounds, and create a life filled with fulfillment, self-acceptance, and meaningful connections. The journey to overcoming childhood struggles is deeply personal, but with awareness, support, and effort, it is entirely possible to heal and thrive.

# Chapter 5: The Role of Emotions in Human Behavior

## How Emotions Drive Our Actions

Emotions are powerful forces that shape our thoughts, behaviors, and decisions. They are deeply intertwined with our instincts and reactions, influencing how we interact with the world and the people around us. While we often think of emotions as fleeting feelings, they are in fact complex physiological and psychological responses that have evolved to help us navigate and adapt to our environment. Understanding how emotions drive our actions can lead to better self-regulation, healthier relationships, and more effective decision-making.

## 1. The Link Between Emotions and Motivation

Emotions are directly tied to motivation, acting as a driving force that propels us toward certain behaviors. When we experience a strong emotion, whether positive or negative, it often prompts us to take action to either pursue a desired outcome or avoid an undesirable one. This motivation is critical in achieving goals, fulfilling needs, and responding to challenges.

- **Positive Emotions and Approach Behavior**: Positive emotions, such as joy, excitement, or satisfaction, motivate us to pursue activities and situations that will bring us pleasure or fulfillment. For example, when someone feels happy or excited about a new opportunity, they may be more inclined to take risks, try new things, or invest effort into pursuing their goals. These emotions signal to us that something is beneficial or rewarding, prompting us to move forward with enthusiasm and optimism.

- **Negative Emotions and Avoidance Behavior**: Negative emotions, such as fear, anger, or sadness, often motivate us to avoid situations that could cause harm or distress. For instance, when we feel fear, we may avoid potentially dangerous or uncomfortable situations. Anger can prompt us to take action to defend ourselves or address perceived injustices. Sadness might motivate us to seek comfort or withdraw from situations that are emotionally painful. While negative emotions can sometimes feel overwhelming, they serve an important protective function by helping us avoid harm and encouraging us to protect our well-being.

## 2. The Role of Emotions in Decision-Making

Our emotional responses play a critical role in decision-making, influencing not only how we process information but also which options we choose to pursue. Emotions can shape our judgments by influencing our perception of risk, reward, and potential outcomes. Understanding the emotional factors involved in decision-making can help individuals make more conscious, thoughtful choices.

- **Emotion-Based Decision-Making**: Research shows that emotions often guide us in making decisions, sometimes even more strongly than logical reasoning. For instance, someone who is feeling anxious may avoid making a decision altogether, fearing the potential negative outcomes. On the other hand, someone who is feeling confident or hopeful may take a leap of faith without fully weighing the risks. While emotions can provide valuable insights and help us make decisions quickly, they can also lead us to make impulsive or irrational choices if we are not aware of how they are influencing us.

- **Emotions and Bias**: Our emotions can create biases in the way we process information, affecting the objectivity of our decisions. For example, when someone is angry, they may perceive situations as more threatening than they actually are, leading to more aggressive or defensive actions. Conversely, feelings of excitement or infatuation can cloud our judgment, leading us to overlook potential risks or negative consequences. Recognizing the emotional influences on our decisions allows us to take a step back, reflect, and consider alternative perspectives before taking action.

## 3. The Influence of Emotions on Social Behavior

Our emotions have a profound impact on how we relate to others. From our interactions with friends and family to our behavior in the workplace, emotions often shape the way we communicate, respond to others, and form connections. Emotional awareness—both of ourselves and others—plays a key role in healthy social functioning.

- **Empathy and Connection**: Positive emotions such as compassion, empathy, and love drive us to connect with others, provide support, and build relationships. When we feel joy or love for someone, we are more likely to show kindness, express affection, and engage in behaviors that strengthen our bonds. Similarly, empathy allows us to tune into the emotions of others, fostering understanding and cooperation. Strong social bonds are often the result of shared emotional experiences, whether through moments of joy, grief, or excitement.

- **Conflict and Emotional Reactions**: On the flip side, negative emotions such as anger, jealousy, or frustration can lead to conflict and hinder communication. For example, when someone feels angry or misunderstood, they may lash out or withdraw, creating distance in their relationships. Similarly, emotions like fear or shame can make individuals less likely to communicate openly or assertively. Emotional intelligence, which involves recognizing and managing one's own emotions as well as understanding others' emotions, plays a crucial role in resolving conflicts and maintaining healthy social interactions.

## 4. The Impact of Unconscious Emotions

Many of the emotions that drive our actions are not consciously recognized, but still profoundly influence our behavior. These unconscious emotions can stem from past experiences, unresolved conflicts, or learned associations, and often lead to automatic responses that we may not fully understand.

- **Implicit Emotions and Automatic Reactions**: Unconscious emotions can trigger automatic reactions, such as avoiding certain people or situations without understanding why. For example, a person who experienced betrayal in the past may feel a strong sense of distrust when faced with a similar situation, even if there is no logical reason to be suspicious. These emotional reactions are often rooted in past experiences and can significantly impact the way we interact with others or make decisions, even when we are not fully aware of them.
- **Emotional Triggers**: Emotional triggers are situations or events that provoke an intense emotional response based on past experiences. For example, someone who experienced childhood trauma might feel anxiety or anger when faced with certain triggers, even though the current situation is not dangerous. Identifying emotional triggers and understanding their origins can help individuals better manage their emotional responses and prevent automatic, reactive behaviors.

## 5. Emotions and Self-Regulation

Self-regulation refers to the ability to manage and control one's emotions, especially in challenging or high-stress situations. The capacity for emotional regulation is a key component of emotional intelligence and is crucial for making thoughtful decisions, maintaining healthy relationships, and achieving personal goals. People who can regulate their emotions are better able to respond to situations in a calm, measured way rather than reacting impulsively.

- **Cognitive Reappraisal**: One effective strategy for regulating emotions is cognitive reappraisal, which involves changing the way we think about a situation in order to alter its emotional impact. For example, instead of viewing a stressful work deadline as a source of anxiety, someone practicing cognitive reappraisal might reframe it as an opportunity to demonstrate their skills and meet a challenge. This shift in perspective can help reduce negative emotions and increase motivation.
- **Mindfulness and Emotional Control**: Mindfulness practices, such as meditation, also help with emotional regulation. By becoming more aware of their emotions as they arise, individuals can pause before reacting and choose more constructive responses. Mindfulness allows for greater emotional clarity, which can lead to better decision-making and healthier interpersonal interactions.

Emotions are not just fleeting feelings—they are powerful drivers of our actions. Whether we are motivated by joy, fear, love, or frustration, our emotional experiences shape how we behave, what decisions we make, and how we relate to others. By understanding the role emotions play in our actions, we can harness their power in positive ways, manage emotional challenges more effectively, and ultimately lead more balanced and fulfilling lives.

# The Science of Emotional Responses

Emotions are complex physiological and psychological reactions that serve as essential signals to help us navigate our environment, respond to challenges, and interact with others. While emotions may feel like personal experiences, they are deeply rooted in our biology and brain function. Understanding the science of emotional responses can provide insights into how emotions are triggered, how they influence our behavior, and how we can better manage and regulate them.

## 1. The Brain and Emotions: The Limbic System

At the heart of emotional responses lies the brain's **limbic system**, which is responsible for processing emotions, memory, and certain behaviors. The limbic system includes several structures, the most important of which are the **amygdala**, **hippocampus**, **hypothalamus**, and **prefrontal cortex**. Each of these areas plays a distinct role in how emotions are experienced and expressed.

- **Amygdala**: The amygdala is often called the "emotion center" of the brain because it is primarily responsible for processing emotional stimuli, particularly those related to fear and danger. When we encounter a stressful or threatening situation, the amygdala rapidly triggers an emotional response, preparing the body for fight or flight. This process happens almost instantly, often before the conscious mind has had a chance to analyze the situation. The amygdala also plays a role in forming emotional memories, helping us remember past experiences linked to strong emotions.
- **Hippocampus**: The hippocampus is closely involved in the storage and retrieval of memories. When an emotional event occurs, the hippocampus helps to connect the emotion with the memory of the experience. This allows emotions to influence how we recall and react to situations in the future. For example, a past traumatic event, such as a car

accident, can trigger feelings of anxiety or fear when we are in similar situations, even if the circumstances are not dangerous.

- **Hypothalamus**: The hypothalamus regulates many of the body's physiological responses to emotions, such as heart rate, blood pressure, and the release of hormones. When we experience strong emotions like fear or excitement, the hypothalamus activates the **autonomic nervous system**, causing changes in bodily functions that prepare us to respond to the situation (e.g., increased heart rate, rapid breathing, or sweating).

- **Prefrontal Cortex**: The prefrontal cortex, located at the front of the brain, plays a crucial role in regulating emotions and making decisions. It helps us evaluate emotional stimuli and decide how to respond. While the amygdala may trigger an emotional response, the prefrontal cortex provides a more rational and thoughtful assessment. It helps us manage emotional impulses, assess consequences, and make appropriate decisions. This is why emotional regulation and decision-making improve as we grow older and gain more control over our emotions.

## 2. Hormones and Neurotransmitters: Chemical Messengers of Emotions

Emotions are not just psychological experiences; they are also driven by a cascade of chemical signals in the brain and body. Hormones and neurotransmitters are the body's chemical messengers that influence emotional responses.

- **Adrenaline (Epinephrine)**: When faced with a threat or high-stress situation, the body releases adrenaline from the adrenal glands. Adrenaline prepares the body for action by increasing heart rate, dilating airways, and boosting blood flow to the muscles. This "fight or flight" response is critical in moments of danger and helps us react quickly. Adrenaline is often associated with emotions like fear, excitement, and anxiety.

- **Cortisol**: Cortisol is another hormone released during stress, often referred to as the "stress hormone." It helps the body respond to stress by increasing glucose availability for energy and regulating the immune system. While short-term cortisol release can be helpful in stressful situations, prolonged or chronic elevation of cortisol levels can lead to negative effects, such as anxiety, depression, and physical health problems like high blood pressure and immune suppression.

- **Oxytocin**: Oxytocin, often called the "love hormone" or "bonding hormone," plays a significant role in social bonding, trust, and affection. It is released during moments of emotional connection, such as hugging, breastfeeding, or during childbirth. Oxytocin promotes feelings of warmth, attachment, and empathy, helping us form social bonds and maintain close relationships.

- **Serotonin**: Serotonin is a neurotransmitter that helps regulate mood, sleep, and appetite. It is often referred to as the "feel-good" neurotransmitter because it promotes feelings of well-being and happiness. Low levels of serotonin have been linked to depression, anxiety, and mood disorders. The balance of serotonin in the brain plays a key role in emotional stability and emotional regulation.

- **Dopamine**: Dopamine is another key neurotransmitter involved in the brain's reward system. It is released when we experience pleasurable activities, such as eating, exercising, or achieving a goal. Dopamine reinforces behaviors that are rewarding, which motivates us to seek out similar experiences in the future. This neurotransmitter plays a role in the experience of joy, satisfaction, and motivation.

## 3. The Physiological Manifestation of Emotions

When we experience an emotion, it's not just our thoughts or brain activity that are affected; our body reacts in ways that are deeply connected to the emotion we're feeling. These physiological responses can include changes in heart rate, breathing, muscle tension, and even body temperature. These changes are part of the body's **autonomic nervous system**, which controls involuntary functions.

- **Fight-or-Flight Response**: In response to fear or stress, the body activates the fight-or-flight response, which involves a surge of energy and heightened alertness. The heart rate increases, blood is redirected to the muscles, and pupils dilate to enhance vision. These physical changes are meant to prepare us to either fight a threat or flee from danger.

- **Rest-and-Digest Response**: In contrast, when we experience emotions like relaxation or contentment, the body switches into the "rest-and-digest" mode, where heart rate and blood pressure decrease, digestion is activated, and the body enters a more peaceful, restful state. This response is associated with positive emotions like calmness and well-being.

- **Facial Expressions and Body Language**: Emotions also manifest in our facial expressions and body language. For example, when we are angry, our facial muscles tense, and our eyebrows furrow. When we are happy, we smile, and our posture may become more open. These expressions often occur involuntarily and can communicate our emotions to others without us having to say a word.

## 4. Emotional Regulation and Coping Strategies

While emotions can be powerful, we also have the ability to manage them. Emotional regulation refers to the strategies we use to influence our emotional experience, expression, and response. This ability is crucial for maintaining mental health and emotional well-being.

- **Cognitive Reappraisal**: One of the most effective ways to regulate emotions is through cognitive reappraisal, which involves changing the way we think about a situation to alter its emotional impact. For example, viewing a stressful situation as an opportunity to grow rather than a threat can reduce anxiety and increase resilience.

- **Mindfulness and Relaxation**: Mindfulness practices, such as meditation and deep breathing, can help calm the body's physiological response to emotions, particularly stress and anxiety. By focusing on the present moment and accepting emotions without judgment, individuals can reduce the intensity of negative emotional experiences.

- **Social Support**: Turning to others for emotional support can also help regulate emotions. Talking to a friend or loved one about our feelings allows us to process emotions, gain perspective, and receive comfort.

By understanding the science behind emotional responses, we can better appreciate the complex interplay between our brain, body, and emotions. This knowledge not only helps us manage emotions more effectively but also fosters emotional intelligence, which improves our relationships and enhances overall well-being.

# Managing Emotions for Better Decisions

Emotions are a fundamental part of human experience, influencing our decisions and shaping our interactions with the world. While emotions can guide us toward making quick, instinctive choices, they can also cloud judgment and lead to impulsive or irrational actions. The ability to manage emotions effectively—especially in high-pressure situations—can enhance decision-making, improve relationships, and promote overall well-being. Understanding the role of emotions in decision-making and learning how to regulate them can help individuals make more balanced, thoughtful choices.

## 1. Recognizing the Influence of Emotions on Decision-Making

Emotions play a crucial role in how we make decisions, often providing immediate feedback that drives us to act. However, they can also create biases that distort our ability to evaluate options objectively. Understanding how emotions influence decision-making is the first step in learning how to manage them effectively.

- **Immediate Emotional Reactions**: When faced with a decision, we often react emotionally before thinking logically. This can lead to snap judgments or actions based on fear, excitement, frustration, or other strong feelings. For instance, if we feel anxious about a particular situation, we may avoid making decisions or postpone important choices out of fear of making a mistake. Alternatively, if we feel excited about an opportunity, we might rush into it without considering the long-term consequences.

- **Emotional Biases**: Our emotions can introduce biases that affect how we perceive situations. For example, **confirmation bias** occurs when we seek out information that aligns with our current emotional state or beliefs, ignoring evidence that contradicts it. Similarly, **overconfidence bias** can arise when we feel overly optimistic or certain about a decision, leading us to overlook potential risks or challenges. Recognizing these biases is key to making better decisions, as it allows us to step back and critically assess our emotional responses.

- **Emotions and Risk-Taking**: Strong emotions like fear, anger, or excitement can either increase or decrease our willingness to take risks. For example, fear may make us overly cautious and hesitant to take action, while anger or excitement can make us more likely to act impulsively. Managing these emotional extremes allows us to assess risk more accurately and make decisions that are aligned with our long-term goals.

## 2. Techniques for Managing Emotions During Decision-Making

While it is natural to feel emotions when making decisions, it is important to regulate them so they do not interfere with our ability to think clearly. By practicing emotional regulation, individuals can make decisions that are more deliberate and balanced, leading to better outcomes.

- **Pause and Reflect**: One of the simplest yet most effective ways to manage emotions is to take a pause before making a decision. In moments of emotional intensity, our initial impulses can be misleading. Taking a step back—whether it's through deep breathing, a short walk, or simply waiting a few moments—gives us time to calm down and regain perspective. This pause helps prevent rash decisions driven by immediate emotional reactions.

- **Cognitive Reframing**: Cognitive reframing is the process of changing the way we perceive a situation in order to manage emotional responses. For example, if you're feeling anxious about a job interview, you might reframe the situation by viewing it as an opportunity to learn and grow, rather than as a source of stress. Reframing allows us to shift our emotional focus and make decisions that are less influenced by fear or anxiety.

- **Mindfulness and Emotional Awareness**: Practicing mindfulness—being fully present in the moment without judgment—can help individuals become more aware of their emotions as they arise. By noticing our emotional reactions without immediately reacting to them, we gain greater control over our responses. Mindfulness techniques, such as meditation, deep breathing, or grounding exercises, can help individuals regulate their emotions and approach decision-making with a clearer mind.

- **Emotional Detachment**: Emotional detachment involves separating ourselves from the emotional charge of a situation to make decisions based on logic and reason rather than emotional impulses. This doesn't mean suppressing emotions or avoiding them entirely, but rather giving ourselves space to assess the situation objectively. For instance, if you're making a financial decision, you might consider both the emotional impact and the practical, long-term consequences of your choices.

- **Consulting Trusted Advisors**: Sometimes, emotions can cloud our judgment to the point where we may not be able to make a clear decision on our own. In such cases, consulting with trusted friends, family, or colleagues can provide an external perspective that is not influenced by the emotional weight of the decision. These advisors can help us see the situation more objectively and offer valuable advice based on experience or logic.

## 3. Building Emotional Intelligence for Better Decision-Making

Emotional intelligence (EQ) refers to the ability to recognize, understand, and manage our own emotions, as well as the emotions of others. High EQ allows individuals to make more thoughtful, informed decisions, as they are better able to assess situations from multiple perspectives and regulate their emotional responses.

- **Self-Awareness**: The foundation of emotional intelligence is self-awareness—the ability to recognize and understand our emotions in real-time. Self-aware individuals are able to identify the emotions influencing their decisions and take steps to manage them effectively. For example, if you recognize that you're feeling frustrated or impatient during a decision-making process, you can take a moment to calm down before proceeding.
- **Self-Regulation**: Self-regulation is the ability to control emotional impulses and reactions, allowing individuals to respond to situations in a calm and measured way. By practicing self-regulation, individuals can avoid making decisions driven by temporary emotions, such as anger or impulsiveness, and instead make choices that align with their long-term goals.

- **Empathy**: Empathy—the ability to understand and share the feelings of others—can also enhance decision-making, especially in interpersonal situations. By considering how others might feel in a given scenario, individuals are better able to make decisions that take everyone's needs and emotions into account. Empathy promotes cooperative decision-making, which can lead to stronger relationships and better outcomes in group settings.
- **Social Skills**: Effective communication and conflict resolution skills are also key components of emotional intelligence that can improve decision-making. Being able to express your thoughts clearly, listen to others, and manage disagreements in a constructive manner helps ensure that decisions are made collaboratively and fairly. This is particularly important in professional or team-based settings where multiple perspectives need to be considered.

In conclusion, emotions are an integral part of the decision-making process, but managing them effectively is crucial to making thoughtful, reasoned choices. By becoming more aware of how emotions influence decisions, learning emotional regulation techniques, and cultivating emotional intelligence, individuals can make better decisions that lead to positive outcomes in both their personal and professional lives.

# Chapter 6: Behavior and Motivation

## What Motivates Us?

Motivation is the driving force behind everything we do, from basic survival instincts to complex behaviors like pursuing goals, forming relationships, and achieving personal growth. Understanding what motivates us—why we act, work, and strive—can provide deeper insights into our behavior and help us harness that energy to reach our potential. Motivation is not a one-size-fits-all concept; it is influenced by a variety of factors, including biological needs, psychological desires, and social influences. These influences can be intrinsic (coming from within) or extrinsic (driven by external factors). Understanding the complexities of motivation is key to understanding ourselves and others, and can help guide more intentional and productive actions.

## 1. Types of Motivation: Intrinsic vs. Extrinsic

Motivation can generally be categorized into two main types: **intrinsic motivation** and **extrinsic motivation**. Both types drive behavior, but they originate from different sources and tend to influence us in different ways.

- **Intrinsic Motivation**: This type of motivation comes from within. It is the desire to engage in an activity for its inherent satisfaction, personal enjoyment, or sense of accomplishment. People who are intrinsically motivated do something because they find it interesting, fulfilling, or meaningful. For example, an artist might paint because it brings them joy and allows them to express their creativity, not because they expect to gain external rewards. Intrinsic motivation is often linked to personal growth, passion, and a deep sense of purpose.

- **Extrinsic Motivation**: This type of motivation is driven by external factors, such as rewards, recognition, or pressure from others. People who are extrinsically motivated engage in activities to achieve a specific outcome or avoid negative consequences. For example, a person may work hard at their job to earn a promotion, receive a paycheck, or gain approval from others. While extrinsic motivation can be powerful, it may not be as sustainable or fulfilling as intrinsic motivation in the long run, as it often depends on external rewards or circumstances that may change over time.

## 2. The Role of Needs in Motivation: Maslow's Hierarchy of Needs

Abraham Maslow's well-known **Hierarchy of Needs** offers a framework for understanding human motivation by categorizing the different levels of needs that drive behavior. According to Maslow, people are motivated by a hierarchy of needs that starts with basic physiological survival needs and progresses to higher psychological and self-fulfillment needs. Understanding these levels helps explain why people pursue different goals and desires at various stages of their lives.

- **Physiological Needs**: These are the most basic human needs, including food, water, shelter, and sleep. At the most fundamental level, humans are motivated to satisfy these needs for survival. When these needs are unmet, they become the primary focus of our behavior.
- **Safety Needs**: Once physiological needs are met, the next priority is safety. This includes physical safety, financial security, and stability. People are motivated to secure their environment and ensure that they

have a safe, predictable existence. This could involve pursuing steady employment, maintaining health insurance, or finding a stable living situation.

- **Love and Belonging Needs**: After safety is secured, humans have an intrinsic need for social connection. We are motivated by the desire to form relationships, friendships, and a sense of belonging. This level of motivation drives behaviors related to family, community, and intimate connections. Feeling loved and accepted is critical for emotional well-being.

- **Esteem Needs**: Once the basic social needs are fulfilled, people are motivated by the need for respect, recognition, and achievement. This includes feelings of self-worth, confidence, and the desire for validation from others. People are driven to gain success in their personal and professional lives, and to be respected and valued by those around them.

- **Self-Actualization**: At the top of Maslow's pyramid is self-actualization— the desire to realize one's full potential, creativity, and personal growth. People who are motivated by self-actualization seek personal fulfillment and the opportunity to express their true selves. This can manifest in pursuing hobbies, furthering education, or engaging in activities that promote self-discovery and improvement.

## 3. The Impact of Emotions on Motivation

Emotions play a significant role in shaping motivation. They are not only a response to external stimuli, but they also influence the choices we make and the actions we take. Emotions can either increase motivation or act as barriers to achieving goals.

- **Positive Emotions as Motivation**: Positive emotions, such as excitement, joy, and pride, can fuel motivation by reinforcing behaviors that lead to rewards or personal satisfaction. For example, feeling pride after completing a challenging project can inspire someone to take on even more ambitious tasks. Similarly, excitement about a new opportunity can drive someone to take risks or explore unfamiliar territory.

- **Negative Emotions and Motivation**: Negative emotions, such as fear, guilt, or frustration, can also serve as powerful motivators. Fear, for example, may motivate someone to act quickly in order to avoid harm or danger. Frustration may push someone to keep trying until they succeed, while guilt can encourage individuals to correct a perceived mistake or make amends in a relationship. However, if not managed properly, negative emotions can be debilitating and lead to avoidance, procrastination, or decision paralysis.

- **Emotion Regulation and Motivation**: The ability to regulate emotions is a key factor in motivation. People who can manage their emotions effectively—particularly negative ones—are better able to stay focused on their goals, overcome setbacks, and persist in the face of challenges. Emotional intelligence, which includes recognizing and controlling emotions, plays a vital role in maintaining motivation and staying on track toward achieving desired outcomes.

## 4. Social and Environmental Influences on Motivation

While intrinsic and extrinsic factors are critical, social and environmental influences can also impact motivation in powerful ways. Our relationships with others, the support we receive, and the environment in which we operate can either amplify or diminish our drive to act.

- **Social Influence and Motivation**: Social support from family, friends, and colleagues can be a significant motivator. Encouragement, praise, and the desire to please others can push people to perform better or achieve more. Additionally, social comparison—comparing oneself to others— can be a motivating factor, especially in competitive environments. However, excessive comparison can also lead to unhealthy pressure or feelings of inadequacy.

- **Environmental Factors**: Our physical and social environments shape the way we feel about our goals. A work environment that is supportive, inspiring, and free of distractions can increase motivation, while a negative or unorganized environment can hinder productivity and engagement. Access to resources, opportunities for growth, and a sense of community can also positively influence motivation levels.

## 5. The Role of Self-Determination Theory

Self-Determination Theory (SDT), developed by psychologists Edward Deci and Richard Ryan, emphasizes the importance of autonomy, competence, and relatedness as core components of motivation. According to SDT, people are most motivated when they feel:

- **Autonomous**: They have control over their actions and decisions, rather than feeling coerced or pressured by external forces.
- **Competent**: They believe in their ability to succeed and feel challenged in a way that fosters growth and mastery.
- **Related**: They feel connected to others, valued, and supported in their endeavors.

When these needs are met, individuals are more likely to be intrinsically motivated, leading to greater satisfaction, persistence, and achievement in both personal and professional pursuits.

# Intrinsic vs. Extrinsic Motivation

Motivation is the force that drives us to take action, whether it's to achieve a goal, complete a task, or pursue an interest. It's essential to understand the difference between **intrinsic** and **extrinsic motivation**, as both types of motivation influence behavior in unique ways. While they often work together, they stem from different sources—internal desires versus external factors—and they shape how we approach tasks, challenges, and rewards.

# 1. Intrinsic Motivation: Driven by Internal Satisfaction

**Intrinsic motivation** refers to the drive to engage in an activity because it is inherently rewarding or enjoyable. When we are intrinsically motivated, the activity itself brings satisfaction, fulfillment, or a sense of accomplishment. This form of motivation is rooted in personal interests, passions, and values, and it does not rely on external rewards or recognition.

**Key Characteristics of Intrinsic Motivation:**

- **Enjoyment and Interest**: People who are intrinsically motivated often engage in an activity because they find it interesting, fun, or engaging. For instance, a musician who plays an instrument simply for the love of making music is intrinsically motivated.
- **Autonomy and Choice**: Intrinsically motivated individuals tend to value the freedom to make their own decisions. The sense of control over their actions and the opportunity to pursue activities that align with their personal interests often enhances their motivation.
- **Personal Growth and Mastery**: Intrinsic motivation is also tied to the desire for self-improvement and personal development. Someone who enjoys solving puzzles or learning new skills does so because the process of mastering something new is rewarding in itself, not necessarily because of an external outcome.
- **Intrinsic Rewards**: The satisfaction that comes from the activity itself is often considered the reward. For example, an artist may paint not for fame or money, but because the act of creating art brings them joy and a sense of personal fulfillment.

**Examples of Intrinsic Motivation:**

- A person who reads a book because they love the subject matter or enjoy reading itself.

- A runner who enjoys the process of running and the physical challenge, rather than running for a prize or medal.
- A student who learns a new language out of personal interest or a desire to connect with a new culture, not for academic grades.

## 2. Extrinsic Motivation: Driven by External Factors

**Extrinsic motivation**, on the other hand, comes from external rewards or pressures. When we are extrinsically motivated, we engage in an activity not because we find it inherently enjoyable or fulfilling, but because we anticipate some form of external payoff, such as money, approval, status, or recognition.

**Key Characteristics of Extrinsic Motivation**:

- **External Rewards**: Extrinsic motivation is driven by tangible rewards such as money, prizes, grades, or promotions. For example, someone may work overtime to earn a bonus, or a student might study hard to get a good grade.
- **Avoidance of Negative Consequences**: Extrinsic motivation can also come from the desire to avoid negative outcomes, such as punishment, criticism, or failure. For instance, an employee may complete a task on time to avoid getting reprimanded by their manager.
- **Social Recognition and Approval**: Often, people are motivated by the desire for recognition, status, or approval from others. A person might pursue a career or academic achievement to impress others or gain social acceptance.
- **Compliance and External Expectations**: Sometimes, extrinsic motivation is driven by external expectations or societal norms. For example, a person might follow the rules, complete a job, or attend school simply because they are expected to do so by society, family, or a specific institution.

**Examples of Extrinsic Motivation**:

- A salesperson working hard to meet a quota for commission.
- A student studying to get high grades or to earn a scholarship.
- An employee working extra hours to receive a promotion or financial incentive.

## 3. The Interaction Between Intrinsic and Extrinsic Motivation

While intrinsic and extrinsic motivation are often seen as opposing forces, they can work together to drive behavior. In many cases, people are motivated by a combination of internal desires and external rewards.

**When Extrinsic Motivation Enhances Intrinsic Motivation**:

- **External rewards can enhance intrinsic motivation if they align with a person's values or personal interests**. For example, a writer who loves to write for the sake of creativity may find external recognition or a publishing deal encouraging, as it affirms the value of their work. Here, the external reward supports the intrinsic motivation rather than replacing it.
- **External encouragement can build confidence**: Praise and positive feedback from others can reinforce intrinsic motivation by affirming a person's abilities or the enjoyment they get from an activity. A student who loves learning may be further motivated by an encouraging teacher who recognizes their efforts.

**When Extrinsic Motivation Undermines Intrinsic Motivation**:

- **Over-reliance on external rewards can diminish intrinsic motivation**: When external rewards are introduced, they can sometimes overshadow the intrinsic enjoyment of an activity. For instance, when a person starts receiving monetary compensation for a hobby they once enjoyed simply for the pleasure of it, they might begin to focus more on the reward than on the activity itself. This can lead to a decrease in motivation to engage in the activity when the external reward is no longer present.

- **External pressure may lead to burnout**: When individuals are constantly motivated by external pressures (e.g., working long hours for a bonus), they may experience stress, anxiety, or burnout, which diminishes their intrinsic desire to perform the task. Over time, the activity can feel like a chore rather than a passion, leading to disengagement.

## 4. Balancing Intrinsic and Extrinsic Motivation

Understanding the balance between intrinsic and extrinsic motivation is key to sustaining long-term motivation. Here are a few strategies for balancing both:

- **Fostering intrinsic motivation**: To maintain long-term motivation, it's important to connect with the intrinsic aspects of an activity. This might mean revisiting why you enjoy the task or how it aligns with your personal goals and values. Focusing on personal growth, mastery, and the joy of the activity can sustain intrinsic motivation.
- **Setting goals and rewards**: Extrinsic motivation can be helpful for short-term goals and as a way to stay on track. However, it's important to set clear, meaningful rewards that align with your intrinsic motivations. For example, setting up a reward system for reaching milestones can provide external incentives, while also reminding you of the deeper personal meaning of the task.
- **Avoid over-reliance on external validation**: While praise and recognition can be motivating, it's important to build intrinsic motivation so that external rewards do not become the sole driver of behavior. If you are only motivated by external validation, you may find yourself less satisfied in the long run.

Understanding the difference between intrinsic and extrinsic motivation helps individuals harness the right kind of energy for different situations. Intrinsic motivation fuels long-term passion and fulfillment, while extrinsic motivation can provide short-term incentives and structure. By learning to balance both types of motivation, we can enhance our ability to achieve personal goals, enjoy our pursuits, and stay motivated in the face of challenges.

# Understanding Why We Do What We Do

Human behavior is complex, and the reasons behind our actions are influenced by a mix of conscious choices, unconscious drives, social influences, and environmental factors. Understanding why we do what we do involves exploring the internal and external motivations that guide our actions, the emotions and cognitive processes that shape them, and the roles of past experiences and social contexts. By delving into these factors, we gain a clearer picture of our behavior, which can help us make better decisions, improve our relationships, and promote personal growth.

## 1. Biological and Physiological Drivers

Our behaviors are strongly influenced by biological and physiological factors, many of which are rooted in our need for survival, comfort, and pleasure. From basic instincts to the more complex interactions of hormones and neurotransmitters, biology plays a crucial role in why we act the way we do.

- **Instincts and Basic Needs**: At the most fundamental level, human actions are often driven by instincts related to survival, reproduction, and the need to meet basic physiological needs. For example, when we feel hungry or thirsty, our behavior is motivated by the need to obtain food or water. Similarly, the drive for shelter, warmth, and safety triggers actions that ensure our survival.

- **Brain Chemistry and Emotions**: Neurotransmitters like dopamine, serotonin, and cortisol play significant roles in influencing our actions. For instance, **dopamine** is associated with reward and pleasure, motivating us to engage in behaviors that bring satisfaction, like eating, exercising, or socializing. On the other hand, **cortisol** is a stress hormone that triggers the body's fight-or-flight response when we encounter danger, influencing how we react in stressful situations.

- **The Role of the Nervous System**: Our nervous system, including the **autonomic nervous system** (ANS), regulates many of the unconscious processes that influence our behavior. The sympathetic division of the ANS activates the "fight or flight" response when we face a perceived threat, motivating us to take action to protect ourselves. The parasympathetic division helps us relax and recover once the threat is removed, encouraging behaviors that restore balance and comfort.

## 2. Psychological Factors: Thoughts, Beliefs, and Perceptions

While our biological makeup lays the foundation for many of our actions, our thoughts, beliefs, and perceptions significantly shape how we interpret and react to the world around us. These psychological factors help us make sense of situations, solve problems, and navigate social interactions.

- **Cognitive Processes**: Our thinking patterns are central to decision-making. For instance, when faced with a decision, we engage in a mental process that weighs potential outcomes, risks, and rewards. These cognitive processes are influenced by past experiences, current emotions, and our ability to focus and analyze information. A person who has had positive experiences with socializing, for example, might actively seek out social interactions, while someone with social anxiety may avoid them.

- **Beliefs and Values**: Our behavior is also shaped by the beliefs and values we hold. These beliefs often come from our upbringing, culture, education, and personal experiences. For example, someone who values independence may prioritize self-reliance in their decision-making and actions, while someone who values community may place a higher importance on group collaboration. These internalized beliefs guide our actions even when we are not consciously aware of them.

- **Perception of Control**: The way we perceive our ability to control a situation can influence our motivation and behavior. People with a high sense of **internal locus of control** believe that they can influence outcomes through their actions, which can lead them to take proactive steps toward achieving their goals. Conversely, individuals with an **external locus of control** may feel that external forces (like luck or fate) control their outcomes, which could lead to passivity or resignation in certain situations.

## 3. Social Influences: The Impact of Others on Our Behavior

Humans are social beings, and much of our behavior is influenced by the people around us. Whether it's our family, friends, colleagues, or broader society, social factors play a critical role in shaping how we act, what we value, and how we interact with the world.

- **Socialization and Family Influence**: From the moment we are born, we are socialized by our families, communities, and cultures. The values, norms, and behaviors we learn in childhood set the stage for how we behave as adults. For instance, a person raised in a family that prioritizes education may be more likely to value learning and pursue academic success. Social norms, like politeness or respect for authority, also shape our behavior within specific cultural contexts.
- **Peer Influence**: Peer pressure and the desire to fit in can strongly influence our behavior, especially during adolescence. The need for social acceptance often drives us to conform to the expectations and behaviors of the groups we belong to, whether it's a circle of friends, coworkers, or online communities. Social identity theory suggests that our sense of belonging to a particular group influences our actions and

attitudes, often motivating us to act in ways that reinforce group cohesion or distinction.

- **Cultural and Societal Expectations**: Broader societal and cultural factors also guide behavior, dictating what is considered acceptable or desirable in various contexts. These influences can shape everything from career choices to family roles and personal relationships. For example, someone living in a culture that emphasizes individual success and achievement may be motivated to work hard to attain personal goals, while in cultures that prioritize collective well-being, behaviors may be more oriented toward collaboration and community.

## 4. The Role of Emotions in Decision-Making and Behavior

Emotions are not just reactions to external stimuli—they also play a powerful role in guiding behavior and decision-making. Our emotions often drive us to take action, whether that's to protect ourselves, pursue a goal, or avoid discomfort.

- **Emotional Reactions**: Emotional responses such as fear, joy, anger, or sadness can be quick and automatic, often prompting us to act before we've had time to think logically. For example, fear can trigger the fight-or-flight response, making us act quickly in response to danger. Positive emotions like excitement or happiness can motivate us to seek out activities that bring pleasure or reward.
- **Emotion and Motivation**: Emotions can provide powerful motivation, either by pushing us toward something we desire or away from something we fear. For instance, someone who feels excited about a new project may be motivated to dedicate time and effort to it, while someone who feels anxious about public speaking may avoid opportunities that require them to perform in front of others. Similarly, emotional discomfort can push people to seek change or improvement in their lives, such as quitting a job they find unfulfilling or leaving an unhealthy relationship.
- **Emotional Regulation**: The ability to regulate emotions is crucial for

managing behavior in a balanced way. People who can recognize and control their emotional responses tend to make more rational, thoughtful decisions. Emotional regulation involves strategies like mindfulness, cognitive reappraisal (changing the way we interpret emotional situations), and emotional expression (constructively channeling feelings rather than suppressing them).

## 5. Past Experiences: How History Shapes Behavior

Our past experiences—especially from childhood and adolescence—play a huge role in shaping our behavior as adults. The lessons we learn from our interactions, successes, failures, and hardships influence our decision-making, emotional responses, and social behavior.

- **Learned Behaviors**: From a young age, we learn how to respond to various situations based on the outcomes of our previous actions. If a child is rewarded for being polite, they are more likely to engage in polite behaviors in the future. Conversely, if a person experiences rejection or failure after taking a certain action, they may be less likely to repeat that behavior, even if the situation calls for it.
- **Trauma and Emotional Memories**: Traumatic experiences, whether physical, emotional, or psychological, can have a lasting impact on behavior. Someone who has experienced betrayal or loss may be more cautious in forming new relationships, while someone who has faced discrimination or hardship may be driven to fight for justice or advocate for others. These emotional memories can guide future decisions, sometimes leading to patterns of avoidance or hypervigilance in certain situations.

## 6. The Complexity of Human Behavior: The Role of Free Will and Adaptability

While many aspects of human behavior are influenced by biological, psychological, and social factors, we also have a degree of agency in how we act. Our ability to make choices, adapt to new circumstances, and learn from experience plays a key role in shaping our behavior over time.

- **Free Will and Choice**: Despite the various influences on our behavior, we still have the capacity to make conscious decisions. Whether we are pursuing a career change, ending an unhealthy habit, or choosing how to respond to stress, our ability to exercise free will allows us to break from old patterns and adopt new behaviors.
- **Adaptability and Growth**: One of the most powerful aspects of human behavior is our ability to adapt. We are constantly learning, growing, and evolving based on our experiences and the changing circumstances of our lives. This adaptability allows us to change our behavior over time, whether in response to new information, shifting environments, or personal growth.

# Chapter 7: Changing Your Behavior

## Identifying Behavioral Patterns You Want to Change

Our behaviors are influenced by a range of factors, from biology and personality to past experiences and social influences. While many of these behaviors serve us well, others can become ingrained over time and may no longer be beneficial. Recognizing the behavioral patterns that are holding you back, causing stress, or leading to undesirable outcomes is the first step toward personal growth and positive change. Identifying these patterns can empower you to take control, adopt healthier habits, and make decisions that align more closely with your goals and values.

## 1. Recognizing Negative or Destructive Behaviors

The first step in identifying behaviors you want to change is to recognize those that are negatively impacting your life. These behaviors may be obvious or subtle, and they can manifest in different areas such as relationships, work, or health. Negative behaviors may be harmful to yourself or others, or they might limit your potential and hinder your progress.

**Common Negative Behaviors to Identify:**

- **Procrastination**: Constantly putting off tasks or delaying important actions can lead to stress, missed opportunities, and a lack of productivity. Procrastination often stems from fear, perfectionism, or a lack of motivation, and can create a cycle of avoidance that is difficult to break.

- **Self-Sabotage**: Engaging in behaviors that undermine your own success—such as avoiding challenges, rejecting opportunities, or actively preventing yourself from reaching your potential—can often be traced back to fear of failure or low self-worth. Self-sabotage can appear in various forms, such as failing to meet deadlines, avoiding important decisions, or neglecting self-care.

- **Unhealthy Coping Mechanisms**: Turning to substances like alcohol, drugs, or food as a way to cope with stress, anxiety, or emotional pain is another behavior to identify. While these behaviors may offer temporary relief, they can have serious long-term consequences for both physical and mental health.

- **Anger or Aggression**: Repeated outbursts of anger or aggressive behavior, whether in personal relationships or at work, can create tension and disrupt communication. Uncontrolled anger often stems from feelings of frustration, insecurity, or unaddressed emotional pain.

- **People-Pleasing**: Constantly seeking approval from others or overextending yourself to meet everyone's needs at the expense of your own well-being can be a pattern driven by a fear of rejection or the need for validation. People-pleasing behaviors can lead to burnout, resentment, and a lack of self-assertiveness.

- **Negative Self-Talk**: If you find yourself consistently thinking or saying things like "I'm not good enough," "I'll never succeed," or "I'm a failure," you may be engaging in negative self-talk. This pattern can affect your confidence, limit your ability to take risks, and hold you back from pursuing new opportunities.

## 2. Tracking Your Behaviors Over Time

Identifying negative or unproductive behaviors often requires a process of self-reflection and awareness. One effective way to gain insight into your behavior patterns is by tracking them over time. Keeping a journal or log can help you pinpoint specific triggers, the emotional states associated with your actions, and the outcomes of your behaviors.

**Ways to Track Your Behaviors**:

- **Daily Journal**: Writing down your thoughts, feelings, and actions throughout the day can help you uncover recurring patterns. Focus on moments when you felt triggered, acted impulsively, or engaged in behaviors you want to change. Over time, patterns will become more apparent.

- **Behavioral Mapping**: Create a visual map of specific situations where you notice unhealthy patterns. For example, track situations where you procrastinate or engage in self-sabotage, and note the context, your emotional state, and the underlying thoughts or beliefs that contributed to your actions.

- **Accountability Partner**: Sharing your goals with a trusted friend, therapist, or coach can provide an external perspective on your behavior. Sometimes, others can spot patterns we miss, and they can offer support or feedback to help you stay on track with your efforts to change.

## 3. Identifying Underlying Beliefs and Thought Patterns

Many behaviors are driven by underlying thoughts, beliefs, and emotions that influence our decisions. Often, these core beliefs are formed in childhood or early experiences and may no longer be valid or helpful. Unpacking these beliefs can reveal why certain behaviors continue to repeat and why change can feel difficult.

**Common Beliefs That Drive Negative Behaviors**:

- **Fear of Failure**: A deep fear of failure can lead to procrastination, self-sabotage, or avoidance of challenges. People with this fear may have internalized the belief that failure is unacceptable or that making mistakes means they are unworthy.

- **Perfectionism**: Believing that you must perform perfectly in every aspect of your life can lead to anxiety, procrastination, and burnout.

Perfectionism is often rooted in a fear of judgment or a desire to gain approval from others.

- **Low Self-Worth**: A belief that you are not good enough or deserving of success can lead to self-sabotage, avoiding opportunities, or under-achieving. This can be triggered by past experiences, critical voices, or unrealistic expectations.

- **People-Pleasing and Approval-Seeking**: The belief that your value depends on the approval or acceptance of others can lead to people-pleasing behaviors, difficulty saying no, and neglecting your own needs.

- **All-or-Nothing Thinking**: Viewing situations in black-and-white terms—such as believing that if you don't succeed completely, you've failed entirely—can lead to avoidance, anxiety, or frustration. This type of thinking can limit your ability to take manageable steps toward progress.

## 4. Observing the Impact of Your Behaviors

To identify which behaviors are worth changing, it's helpful to observe their impact on your life and the lives of others. Consider both the short-term and long-term consequences of your actions. While certain behaviors might provide temporary relief or rewards, they can be detrimental over time.

- **Emotional Impact**: Does the behavior leave you feeling drained, anxious, or regretful? For example, overworking might give you a sense of accomplishment in the short term but could lead to burnout, stress, and emotional exhaustion in the long run.

- **Relationships**: How do your behaviors affect your relationships with others? Patterns like people-pleasing or anger can cause strain in personal and professional relationships, leading to feelings of resentment or miscommunication.

- **Physical and Mental Health**: Pay attention to how your behaviors impact your physical and mental health. For instance, unhealthy coping mechanisms like overeating or excessive drinking may provide temporary relief but can lead to long-term health problems, low energy, or poor mental health.

## 5. Reflecting on Past Experiences and Habit Formation

Our behaviors often stem from habits formed over time, influenced by past experiences, cultural conditioning, and learned responses. Understanding how these patterns became entrenched can shed light on why they are hard to change and provide clues for how to break them.

- **Past Experiences**: Reflect on your upbringing, childhood experiences, and significant life events. Often, behaviors such as people-pleasing, perfectionism, or fear of rejection are tied to early experiences where you learned to seek approval or avoid conflict. Understanding the root cause of these patterns can help you address them more effectively.
- **Habit Loops**: Behaviors often become ingrained into habits—automatic responses to certain triggers or situations. Identifying the cues that lead to these habitual behaviors, along with the rewards or relief they provide, can help you change the cycle. For example, if stress triggers procrastination, learning to manage stress more effectively can help you break the habit of delaying tasks.

By identifying behavioral patterns you want to change, you gain the clarity needed to take proactive steps toward growth. This self-awareness allows you to focus on changing the behaviors that no longer serve you, ultimately leading to a healthier, more fulfilling life.

# Techniques for Personal Growth to Change

Personal growth is an ongoing process that involves developing self-awareness, learning new skills, and making conscious efforts to improve various aspects of your life. Changing deeply ingrained habits or behaviors can be challenging, but with the right tools and mindset, it is entirely achievable. Here are several techniques that can help you break free from negative patterns and foster lasting personal growth.

## 1. Self-Reflection and Awareness

The first step in personal growth is becoming more aware of your thoughts, feelings, and behaviors. Self-reflection allows you to identify patterns and gain clarity on the areas of your life that need change. By understanding the root causes of your behavior, you can better address the underlying issues and create a plan for improvement.

**Techniques for Self-Reflection**:

- **Journaling**: Writing about your experiences, thoughts, and emotions regularly can provide insights into your internal world. Journaling helps you track your progress, recognize patterns in your behavior, and reflect on situations where you want to change. It can also serve as a tool for processing difficult emotions or stressful events.
- **Mindfulness and Meditation**: Practicing mindfulness helps you become more aware of your thoughts and feelings in the present moment without judgment. Meditation can deepen this practice, allowing you to observe your emotions, habits, and reactions more objectively. Mindfulness can also help reduce impulsivity and increase emotional regulation, which is essential for making thoughtful decisions.
- **Feedback from Others**: Asking trusted friends, family members, or colleagues for feedback can provide an external perspective on your behavior. Constructive feedback helps you recognize blind spots and identify areas where you may need to make changes.

## 2. Setting Clear and Achievable Goals

One of the most effective ways to foster personal growth is to set specific, measurable, and achievable goals. Setting clear goals gives you a sense of direction and purpose, making it easier to stay motivated and focused on the changes you want to make.

**Steps to Setting Effective Goals**:

- **Define Your Vision**: Begin by thinking about your long-term vision for your life. What kind of person do you want to become? What habits do you want to develop or eliminate? Having a clear vision of where you want to go helps guide your goals and makes the process of change feel more meaningful.
- **Break Down Goals into Smaller Steps**: Once you have a larger goal in mind, break it down into smaller, actionable steps. For example, if your goal is to develop better time management skills, you might break this down into smaller actions such as creating a daily schedule, setting priorities, or minimizing distractions.
- **Track Your Progress**: Regularly monitor your progress toward your goals. Celebrate small successes along the way to stay motivated and adjust your approach if necessary. Tracking your progress keeps you accountable and allows you to identify areas that need more attention.

## 3. Building Healthy Habits

Changing behavior requires replacing old, unhealthy habits with new, more positive ones. The process of habit formation can take time, but with consistency and persistence, new habits can become automatic.

**Techniques for Building New Habits**:

- **Start Small**: Begin by focusing on one habit at a time. Trying to overhaul your entire life all at once can feel overwhelming and unsustainable. Choose a single behavior to focus on and gradually build from there. For example, if you want to exercise more, start with short daily workouts and gradually increase the intensity and duration.

- **Create a Routine**: Consistency is key when forming new habits. Integrate your desired behaviors into your daily routine to make them a regular part of your life. The more frequently you practice a new habit, the more likely it will become ingrained in your lifestyle.
- **Use Reminders and Triggers**: Use external cues to remind you to perform your new habit. For example, you can place a water bottle on your desk as a reminder to stay hydrated or set a phone reminder to practice mindfulness each day. Positive triggers, such as a reward after completing a task, can reinforce the habit-forming process.

## 4. Overcoming Obstacles and Negative Self-Talk

During the process of personal growth, it's natural to encounter obstacles, setbacks, and moments of doubt. Negative self-talk can undermine your progress and make it harder to stay on track. Learning to recognize and challenge these negative thoughts is crucial for creating lasting change.

**Techniques to Overcome Negative Self-Talk**:

- **Cognitive Behavioral Therapy (CBT)**: CBT is a therapeutic approach that helps individuals identify and change negative thought patterns. By recognizing distorted thinking (e.g., "I'm not good enough" or "I'll never change") and replacing it with more balanced, realistic thoughts, you can improve your self-esteem and maintain a positive outlook.
- **Positive Affirmations**: Replacing negative self-talk with positive affirmations can boost confidence and motivation. Repeating affirmations like "I am capable of change" or "I have the strength to achieve my goals" helps reframe your mindset and promotes self-belief.
- **Visualization**: Visualization involves imagining yourself successfully achieving your goals and engaging in the desired behavior. By vividly picturing success, you create a mental roadmap that strengthens your commitment and reinforces positive thinking.

## 5. Practicing Patience and Self-Compassion

Personal growth is a journey, not a destination. Change takes time, and it is important to practice patience with yourself throughout the process. When setbacks occur (and they will), it's essential to approach yourself with self-compassion rather than self-criticism.

**How to Practice Patience and Self-Compassion:**

- **Embrace Imperfection**: Recognize that no one is perfect, and personal growth involves trial and error. Instead of focusing on mistakes or failures, view them as learning opportunities that bring you closer to your goals.
- **Be Kind to Yourself**: Treat yourself with the same kindness and understanding that you would offer a friend. If you slip up or encounter difficulties, don't beat yourself up. Acknowledge the setback, learn from it, and continue moving forward with renewed determination.
- **Celebrate Progress, Not Perfection**: Focus on the progress you've made, even if it feels small. Each step forward is an achievement, and celebrating these milestones can boost your confidence and motivation to continue.

## 6. Seeking Support and Accountability

Changing deeply ingrained behaviors is often easier with support. Whether it's from a mentor, friend, therapist, or support group, having someone to encourage you, provide feedback, and hold you accountable can increase your chances of success.

**Ways to Seek Support:**

- **Accountability Partner**: Having an accountability partner who shares similar goals or is invested in your success can provide motivation and help you stay on track. Regular check-ins and discussions can reinforce your commitment to change.

- **Therapy or Coaching**: Working with a professional, such as a therapist or life coach, can provide structure and guidance as you work through personal challenges. These professionals can help you identify deep-seated issues, develop strategies for change, and offer emotional support throughout the process.
- **Join a Group or Community**: Support groups or online communities can offer encouragement and shared experiences. Connecting with others who are on a similar path can provide valuable insights and emotional support.

By utilizing these techniques for personal growth, you can gradually shift patterns of behavior that no longer serve you, build healthier habits, and create a more fulfilling and intentional life. Change is a process, and with the right strategies and mindset, you can overcome obstacles and grow into the person you aspire to be.

# Developing Healthy Habits and Breaking Bad Ones

Healthy habits are the foundation of a fulfilling and productive life, while bad habits can hold us back and negatively impact our physical, emotional, and mental well-being. Habits are automatic behaviors that form over time through repetition, making them difficult to change. However, with a strategic and consistent approach, you can replace bad habits with healthier ones that align with your goals and values.

# 1. Understanding How Habits Form

To develop healthy habits or break bad ones, it's important to understand the science of habit formation. Habits are formed through a three-step process known as the **habit loop**, which includes a **cue**, a **routine**, and a **reward**:

- **Cue**: The trigger that initiates the behavior. For example, feeling stressed might cue you to reach for comfort food, or seeing your running shoes might remind you to exercise.
- **Routine**: The behavior itself, which could be positive (exercising) or negative (eating junk food).
- **Reward**: The benefit or relief you feel after performing the behavior. The brain associates this reward with the cue, reinforcing the habit over time.

Understanding this loop can help you identify the triggers of your bad habits and design strategies to develop healthier alternatives.

# 2. Steps to Developing Healthy Habits

Creating healthy habits involves replacing old routines with new, beneficial behaviors. The key is to make the process as simple and rewarding as possible.
### a. Start Small

- Begin with a single, manageable change to avoid feeling overwhelmed. For instance, instead of committing to a one-hour workout every day, start with a 10-minute walk. Small, achievable goals build momentum and confidence over time.

### b. Identify Your "Why"

- Understand the deeper reason behind your desire to build a new habit. For example, if you want to eat healthier, your motivation might be to feel more energetic or reduce health risks. A clear sense of purpose helps you stay committed when motivation wanes.

### c. Create a Cue

- Use triggers to remind you to perform your new habit. For instance, leave a water bottle on your desk to encourage hydration, or place workout clothes by your bed to prompt morning exercise. Linking your habit to an existing routine, like brushing your teeth or drinking coffee, can also help establish consistency.

### d. Make It Easy

- Simplify the process of building a new habit by removing barriers. For example, prepare healthy meals in advance, set up an automatic savings plan, or download an app to track your progress. The easier the habit is to perform, the more likely you'll stick to it.

### e. Reward Yourself

- Reinforce your new habit by attaching a reward to it. For example, after completing a workout, treat yourself to a relaxing bath or listen to your favorite podcast. Rewards help your brain associate the habit with positive feelings, making it more likely to stick.

### f. Track Your Progress

- Monitoring your progress keeps you motivated and accountable. Use a journal, app, or calendar to track each time you perform the habit. Seeing your progress builds momentum and gives you a sense of accomplishment.

# 3. Strategies for Breaking Bad Habits

Breaking bad habits requires disrupting the habit loop by altering the cue, routine, or reward. The goal is to replace negative behaviors with healthier alternatives that fulfill the same need.

### a. Identify the Cue

- Pay attention to the triggers that lead to your bad habit. Is it stress, boredom, certain environments, or specific people? For example, if you notice that you snack on unhealthy food when you're stressed, the cue is stress.

### b. Replace the Routine

- Substitute a healthier behavior for the bad habit. For example:
- If stress prompts you to eat junk food, replace the routine with taking a short walk or practicing deep breathing exercises.
- If boredom leads you to scroll on your phone for hours, try reading a book or doing a creative activity instead.

### c. Change Your Environment

- Altering your environment can help disrupt the cues associated with bad habits. For instance, remove tempting junk food from your home or limit your screen time by keeping your phone in another room during work hours. A supportive environment makes it easier to resist old patterns.

### d. Delay Gratification

- When you feel the urge to engage in a bad habit, delay the behavior for a few minutes. This small pause gives you time to reconsider your actions and choose a healthier alternative. Often, the urge will pass if you wait long enough.

## e. Use Negative Consequences

- Introduce consequences that discourage bad habits. For example, enlist a friend to hold you accountable or set penalties for yourself, like donating to a cause you don't support if you break your commitment.

## f. Practice Self-Compassion

- Breaking a bad habit takes time, and setbacks are normal. Instead of criticizing yourself for slipping up, reflect on what triggered the behavior and use it as a learning opportunity. A positive mindset makes it easier to stay on track.

# 4. Leveraging Accountability and Support

Building healthy habits and breaking bad ones is easier with support from others. Accountability helps you stay consistent and motivated, especially during challenging moments.

- **Accountability Partners**: Share your goals with a trusted friend or family member who can check in with you regularly. Having someone to encourage you and celebrate your progress makes the process more rewarding.
- **Support Groups or Communities**: Joining a group of like-minded individuals with similar goals can provide encouragement and inspiration. Whether it's a fitness class, book club, or online forum, connecting with others reinforces your commitment.
- **Professional Guidance**: If you're struggling with deeply ingrained habits, consider working with a therapist, coach, or mentor. These professionals can offer tailored strategies and emotional support to help you succeed.

# 5. Building Resilience Against Setbacks

Both habit formation and breaking bad habits require resilience and persistence. Setbacks are a natural part of the process, but they don't have to derail your progress.

## a. Learn from Setbacks

- When a setback occurs, reflect on what triggered it and how you can handle similar situations differently in the future. For example, if stress caused you to skip a workout, plan to schedule exercise earlier in the day or incorporate relaxation techniques into your routine.

## b. Focus on Progress, Not Perfection

- Instead of aiming for perfection, celebrate small wins and incremental improvements. Consistency matters more than perfection when it comes to building lasting habits.

## c. Reassess and Adjust

- Periodically evaluate your habits and goals to ensure they still align with your priorities. Adjust your approach if necessary to keep your progress sustainable and meaningful.

# 6. The Power of Positive Reinforcement

Positive reinforcement is one of the most effective tools for solidifying new habits. Rewarding yourself for progress and celebrating milestones reinforces the connection between your behavior and the positive outcomes it produces.

**Ways to Use Positive Reinforcement**:

- Treat yourself to something you enjoy, like a favorite meal or a relaxing activity, after reaching a goal.

- Acknowledge your progress with a visual tracker, like a habit calendar or app.
- Share your achievements with others who can celebrate your success with you.

By focusing on the rewards and benefits of healthy habits, you strengthen your motivation to maintain them over the long term.

Through self-awareness, consistency, and strategic effort, you can create positive habits that enrich your life while breaking free from negative ones. Healthy habits provide a foundation for growth, resilience, and fulfillment, empowering you to achieve your goals and live a more intentional life.

# Chapter 8: Overcoming Limiting Beliefs

## How Beliefs Shape Our Actions

Our beliefs—whether they are about ourselves, others, or the world around us—have a profound impact on how we think, feel, and behave. Beliefs act as a lens through which we interpret our experiences, and they influence the decisions we make, how we respond to challenges, and the way we interact with others. Understanding how beliefs shape our actions is crucial for personal growth, as it allows us to examine the unconscious patterns that drive our behavior and make intentional changes when necessary.

## 1. The Power of Self-Beliefs

The beliefs we hold about ourselves, often referred to as **self-beliefs**, play a significant role in shaping our actions and behaviors. These beliefs influence our self-esteem, confidence, and the goals we set for ourselves.

**Self-Efficacy and Confidence**

- **Self-efficacy** refers to the belief in our ability to accomplish specific tasks or achieve certain goals. Those who believe in their own capabilities are more likely to take on challenges, persist through difficulties, and succeed in their efforts. For example, someone with high self-efficacy in their professional skills may seek out new opportunities for growth and advancement. On the other hand, someone with low self-efficacy might avoid challenges, fearing failure or believing they are not capable of success.

- **Confidence** plays a similar role in motivating behavior. If you believe you can handle a situation—whether it's a public speaking event or a difficult project—you are more likely to take the necessary steps to prepare and succeed. Conversely, if you doubt your abilities, you may shy away from those situations, often missing opportunities for growth.

**Self-Worth and Motivation**

- The belief in our own worth influences how we treat ourselves and others. When we believe we are worthy of success, love, or happiness, we are more likely to pursue goals, form healthy relationships, and take actions that align with our values. People with low self-worth, however, may engage in self-destructive behaviors or avoid taking risks due to a fear of rejection or failure. Their actions often stem from a belief that they don't deserve to succeed or be happy.

## 2. Beliefs About the World and Others

Our perceptions of the world around us, including our beliefs about other people and society, shape how we engage with our environment. These beliefs can influence everything from our relationships to the way we approach challenges in life.

**Social Beliefs and Interactions**

- **Trust and Relationships**: If you believe that people are generally trustworthy, you are more likely to form positive, open relationships with others. Trust allows for deeper connections and collaboration. On the other hand, if you believe that people are unreliable or dishonest, you may become more guarded, distant, and cynical, limiting your ability to form meaningful relationships.

- **Cultural and Societal Beliefs**: Cultural beliefs shape how we interact with others and perceive societal norms. For example, if you hold the belief that success is defined by material wealth, you might prioritize career achievements or financial goals over personal well-being or relationships. Alternatively, if you believe that happiness is rooted in family and community, you may place a higher value on nurturing those aspects of life.

**Growth Mindset vs. Fixed Mindset**

- People with a **growth mindset** believe that abilities and intelligence can be developed through effort, learning, and perseverance. This belief leads them to embrace challenges, learn from failures, and continuously improve themselves. As a result, they are more likely to take proactive steps toward personal development and success.
- Those with a **fixed mindset**, on the other hand, believe that their abilities are static and cannot be changed. They may avoid challenges to protect their sense of competence, fearing that failure will expose their limitations. This belief often leads to stagnation and avoidance of opportunities for growth.

## 3. How Beliefs Influence Decision-Making and Behavior

Beliefs act as filters that shape the way we evaluate situations and make decisions. Our beliefs about the outcomes of our actions influence how we approach choices, risk, and uncertainty.

**Risk Perception and Behavior**

- If you believe that taking risks will lead to failure or negative consequences, you may avoid taking chances, even when opportunities for growth or reward are present. This belief can lead to missed opportunities and limit personal or professional progress. Conversely, if you believe that risks are necessary for growth and success, you are more likely to take calculated risks that could open doors to new possibilities.

**Beliefs About Control**

- Beliefs about control—specifically, the degree to which we believe we have control over our lives—can significantly affect our actions. If you have an **internal locus of control**, you believe that your actions and decisions directly influence outcomes in your life. This belief tends to foster self-discipline, motivation, and responsibility.
- In contrast, if you have an **external locus of control**, you believe that external forces, such as luck, fate, or the actions of others, are responsible for the outcomes in your life. This belief can lead to a passive approach to life, where you may feel helpless or less motivated to take charge of your circumstances.

## 4. Beliefs and Behavioral Change

Our beliefs are not fixed—they can evolve over time based on new experiences, information, and self-reflection. Changing limiting or negative beliefs is a key step in achieving personal growth and improving behavior.

- **Cognitive Restructuring**: This technique involves identifying and challenging negative or unhelpful beliefs, then replacing them with more positive, realistic ones. For example, if you believe "I'm not good enough to succeed," you can reframe it to "I have the ability to learn and grow through effort." This shift in belief can encourage a more proactive approach to challenges.
- **Reinforcing Positive Beliefs**: Positive affirmations, visualization, and setting small, achievable goals can help reinforce empowering beliefs. When you see evidence that your beliefs are leading to positive outcomes, it strengthens your motivation and encourages more constructive behaviors.

Understanding how beliefs shape our actions provides insight into why we behave the way we do, and how we can change our behavior by altering the beliefs that drive it. By identifying limiting or negative beliefs and replacing them with more empowering ones, we can transform not only how we perceive ourselves but also how we act in the world.

# Identifying and Challenging Self-Limiting Beliefs

Self-limiting beliefs are deeply ingrained thoughts or convictions that constrain our potential, prevent us from pursuing our goals, or keep us stuck in patterns of behavior that do not serve us. These beliefs, often formed from past experiences or societal conditioning, tend to hold us back by creating false narratives about what we can and cannot achieve. Identifying and challenging these beliefs is a key step in personal growth, as it allows us to break free from the mental barriers that hinder our success and fulfillment.

## 1. Understanding Self-Limiting Beliefs

Self-limiting beliefs are often unconscious, meaning we may not always recognize when they are influencing our decisions or actions. They tend to arise from fear, past failures, negative feedback, or societal expectations. These beliefs can manifest in various ways, such as thoughts like "I'm not good enough," "I'll never succeed," or "I'm not deserving of happiness."

**Common Types of Self-Limiting Beliefs**:

- **Imposter Syndrome**: The belief that you are not as competent or deserving as others think you are, despite evidence of success.
- **Fear of Failure**: The belief that failure is not only inevitable but also

catastrophic, leading to avoidance of new opportunities or challenges.

- **Perfectionism**: The belief that you must be perfect in every task, and anything less than flawless is a failure.
- **Unworthiness**: The belief that you do not deserve success, happiness, or love, often stemming from past experiences of rejection or criticism.
- **Limiting Identity**: The belief that your current identity or past experiences define what you can achieve. For instance, believing that because you're introverted, you can't be successful in social or leadership roles.

## 2. Identifying Self-Limiting Beliefs

The first step in overcoming self-limiting beliefs is to recognize and bring them to the surface. Because these beliefs are often deeply ingrained, it can take some time to become aware of them. However, through careful self-reflection and mindfulness, you can begin to identify the beliefs that are holding you back.

**Techniques for Identifying Self-Limiting Beliefs**:

- **Self-Reflection**: Take time to reflect on the thoughts, feelings, and behaviors that occur when you face challenges or pursue goals. Are there recurring patterns of doubt or fear? Do you often find yourself giving up before you even try, or do you avoid new opportunities out of fear? Journaling can be a powerful tool for uncovering self-limiting beliefs, as it allows you to track your thoughts and identify negative patterns.
- **Mindfulness and Awareness**: Becoming more aware of your thoughts and emotional responses in real-time can help you catch self-limiting beliefs as they arise. For example, when you feel fear or resistance towards an opportunity, take a moment to ask yourself, "What belief is driving this reaction?" Is it the belief that you will fail or that you are not capable of succeeding?
- **Feedback from Others**: Sometimes, our self-limiting beliefs can be difficult to see on our own. Asking trusted friends, family members, or

colleagues for feedback can help you identify areas where you may be holding yourself back. They may notice patterns or behaviors that you are too close to recognize.

- **Examine Patterns of Behavior**: Take note of recurring patterns of self-sabotage, procrastination, or avoidance. These behaviors often stem from underlying self-limiting beliefs. For example, if you consistently avoid public speaking opportunities, it may be because of the belief that you are not articulate enough or fear judgment.

## 3. Challenging Self-Limiting Beliefs

Once you have identified your self-limiting beliefs, the next step is to challenge them. Simply recognizing these beliefs is not enough; you must actively work to question and replace them with healthier, more empowering beliefs.

**Techniques for Challenging Self-Limiting Beliefs**:

- **Question the Evidence**: One of the most powerful ways to challenge a self-limiting belief is to ask yourself, "What evidence do I have for this belief?" Often, these beliefs are based on assumptions or past experiences that may no longer be relevant. For example, if you believe you're not good enough for a promotion, examine your track record—what accomplishments or positive feedback suggest otherwise? Challenging the evidence behind your beliefs can reveal the flaws in your thinking.
- **Reframe the Belief**: Reframing is the process of looking at a belief from a different perspective. For instance, if you hold the belief that "failure is bad," you could reframe it as "failure is an opportunity to learn and grow." Shifting your perspective allows you to view challenges and setbacks as part of the growth process rather than as barriers to success.
- **Affirmations and Positive Self-Talk**: Replacing self-limiting beliefs with positive affirmations can help reprogram your mind over time. Affirmations are positive, present-tense statements that challenge the negative beliefs you hold. For example, if you believe you are not capable of success, you might repeat, "I am capable and worthy of success" or

"I have the skills and perseverance to achieve my goals." Consistently practicing positive self-talk reinforces new, empowering beliefs.

- **Visualize Success**: Visualization is a powerful tool for changing self-limiting beliefs. When you visualize yourself achieving your goals, you create a mental image of success that contradicts the limiting beliefs you hold. Visualization can help you develop the confidence and belief that you are capable of succeeding. For example, if you have a fear of public speaking, visualize yourself speaking confidently in front of an audience and receiving positive feedback.

- **Take Action**: Challenging self-limiting beliefs is not just about changing your thoughts; it's also about taking action. By taking small steps toward your goals, you can prove to yourself that your self-limiting beliefs are not true. Each successful step, no matter how small, strengthens the new belief that you are capable of achieving what you set out to do. For example, if you believe you are bad at networking, start by attending one event, and gradually build your confidence through experience.

- **Seek Support**: Sometimes, breaking through self-limiting beliefs requires external support. Working with a therapist, coach, or mentor can provide guidance and help you reframe your thinking. Support groups or community forums can also offer encouragement and validation as you challenge your beliefs and make positive changes in your life.

## 4. Cultivating a Growth Mindset

At the core of challenging self-limiting beliefs is cultivating a **growth mindset**—the belief that abilities and intelligence can be developed through effort and learning. A growth mindset encourages you to view challenges as opportunities for growth rather than insurmountable obstacles. By embracing the idea that you can improve through dedication and hard work, you begin to let go of limiting beliefs and replace them with a mindset focused on progress, resilience, and self-improvement.

By identifying and challenging your self-limiting beliefs, you can break free from the constraints that hold you back, allowing you to pursue your goals and unlock your full potential. This process is not always easy, but with persistence and the right tools, it is possible to transform the way you think and act, leading to lasting change.

# Building a Growth-Oriented Mindset

A growth-oriented mindset, often referred to as a **growth mindset**, is the belief that abilities and intelligence can be developed through dedication, hard work, and learning from mistakes. This mindset contrasts with a **fixed mindset**, where individuals believe their talents and intelligence are static traits that cannot change. Adopting a growth mindset can be a powerful tool for personal development, as it encourages resilience, adaptability, and the belief that challenges are opportunities for learning rather than obstacles to success. Building a growth-oriented mindset can transform the way we approach challenges, setbacks, and even everyday tasks.

## 1. Understanding the Growth Mindset

The concept of a growth mindset was popularized by psychologist **Carol Dweck**. She discovered that individuals with a growth mindset are more likely to embrace challenges, persist in the face of difficulties, and see effort as a necessary part of mastery. In contrast, those with a fixed mindset tend to avoid challenges, give up easily, and believe that failure reflects their inherent lack of ability.

**Key Characteristics of a Growth-Oriented Mindset:**

- **Embracing Challenges**: People with a growth mindset view challenges as opportunities to learn and grow. Instead of avoiding difficult tasks, they tackle them head-on, knowing that the process will improve their skills and knowledge.

- **Learning from Feedback**: Individuals with a growth mindset are open to feedback, seeing it as a valuable tool for improvement rather than a judgment of their abilities. Constructive criticism is viewed as a way to refine and better understand their weaknesses.
- **Persistence in the Face of Setbacks**: Rather than giving up after failure, those with a growth mindset understand that setbacks are part of the learning process. They are more likely to try again, adapt their strategies, and persist until they succeed.
- **The Power of Effort**: A key belief of a growth-oriented mindset is that effort is essential for improvement. Individuals with this mindset understand that talent alone is not enough; sustained effort and practice are needed to achieve mastery.

## 2. Shifting from a Fixed to a Growth Mindset

If you have a fixed mindset, the good news is that you can change it. Cultivating a growth-oriented mindset takes time and intentional effort, but it is achievable through consistent practice and reflection. Here are some practical strategies for making the shift.

### a. Recognize and Challenge Fixed Mindset Thoughts

- The first step to building a growth mindset is identifying when you're thinking with a fixed mindset. These thoughts might include statements like "I'm just not good at this," "I'll never be able to do that," or "I'm too old to learn something new." When these thoughts arise, challenge them by reframing them into more growth-oriented statements. For example, instead of saying "I'm terrible at this," you might say, "I'm not good at this yet, but with practice, I can improve."

### b. Focus on the Process, Not Just the Outcome

- In a growth mindset, the emphasis is on effort and the learning process rather than just the results. Rather than focusing solely on winning or achieving an end goal, shift your attention to the progress you're making along the way. Celebrate small victories and improvements, no matter how minor they may seem.

## c. Embrace Challenges and Step Out of Your Comfort Zone

- A growth mindset thrives on challenges. Start seeking out opportunities that stretch your abilities. This might mean taking on a more difficult project at work, learning a new skill, or tackling something you've been avoiding out of fear. The more you challenge yourself, the more you expand your comfort zone and the more you will grow.

## d. Learn from Mistakes and Failures

- Mistakes and failures are inevitable, but in a growth-oriented mindset, they are not seen as roadblocks—they're seen as valuable learning experiences. Instead of feeling defeated by failure, reflect on what went wrong and what you can learn from the situation. Ask yourself, "What could I do differently next time?" or "What did I learn that will help me improve?" By adopting this mindset, failure becomes a necessary part of growth rather than something to fear or avoid.

# 3. Cultivating a Love for Learning

A key component of a growth-oriented mindset is a deep love for learning. People with a growth mindset are intrinsically motivated to improve their skills, expand their knowledge, and embrace new experiences. Cultivating this love for learning can help you remain curious, adaptable, and open to change.

**Techniques for Cultivating a Growth-Oriented Love for Learning:**

- **Pursue Lifelong Learning**: Make learning a habit. Take classes, read books, attend workshops, and explore topics that interest you. Even if the subject isn't directly related to your career or goals, the act of learning will reinforce the idea that growth and development are continual processes.
- **Seek New Experiences**: Challenge yourself to try new things regularly. Whether it's learning a new language, picking up a new hobby, or exploring a new culture, stepping outside your comfort zone and embracing novelty reinforces the idea that growth is an ongoing journey.
- **Celebrate Curiosity**: Approach life with curiosity, asking questions and seeking out answers. Embrace the idea that you don't need to know everything right now and that discovery is part of the process.

## 4. Surround Yourself with Growth-Oriented Influences

The people you interact with can play a significant role in fostering or hindering a growth-oriented mindset. Surrounding yourself with individuals who have a growth mindset can provide inspiration, support, and accountability. **Ways to Build a Growth-Oriented Support System**:

- **Seek Mentors**: Find individuals who exemplify a growth mindset and learn from them. Mentors can offer valuable advice, share their own experiences, and challenge you to push past your limits.
- **Join Communities with a Growth Mindset**: Engage in communities or groups that prioritize learning, personal growth, and improvement. These environments will reinforce the idea that growth is continuous and will encourage you to keep striving.
- **Stay Away from Toxic Influences**: Be mindful of people who have a fixed mindset or are overly critical, as their negative attitudes may hinder your progress. Surround yourself with those who encourage and inspire you to take risks and grow.

## 5. Practice Self-Compassion and Patience

Developing a growth-oriented mindset requires patience and self-compassion. There will be setbacks and moments of frustration along the way, but the key is to remain kind to yourself during the process. Growth takes time, and it's important to celebrate your progress and be gentle with yourself when things don't go as planned.

# Chapter 9: The Power of Self-Awareness

## Understanding Your Own Behavior

Understanding your own behavior is a crucial aspect of personal growth and emotional intelligence. Our actions, thoughts, and emotions are shaped by a complex mix of internal factors (like beliefs, desires, and past experiences) and external influences (such as societal norms, relationships, and environments). By developing self-awareness and examining the underlying causes of your behavior, you can gain greater control over your actions, make better decisions, and create positive changes in your life.

## 1. Self-Awareness: The First Step to Understanding Behavior

Self-awareness is the ability to observe and reflect on your thoughts, feelings, and actions without judgment. It's the foundation of understanding your behavior because it allows you to recognize patterns, motivations, and triggers. Without self-awareness, it's easy to act on impulse, react defensively, or fall into automatic habits that may not be serving you well.

**Practices to Enhance Self-Awareness:**

- **Mindfulness**: Practicing mindfulness helps you stay present in the moment, noticing your thoughts and feelings as they arise. By observing without judgment, you can gain insights into what drives your behavior in any given situation.

- **Journaling**: Writing down your thoughts and experiences regularly can help you identify recurring patterns in your behavior. It allows you to process your emotions and reflect on your actions, helping you see connections between your feelings and your actions.
- **Meditation**: Meditation is another powerful tool for fostering self-awareness. It helps you quiet the mind, create distance from your thoughts, and understand the underlying motivations driving your behavior.

## 2. The Role of Emotions in Behavior

Our emotions play a huge role in shaping our actions. Whether we're aware of it or not, our feelings influence how we respond to situations, how we interact with others, and how we perceive the world. Emotions can trigger automatic responses or thoughtful reactions, but they always play a part in guiding our behavior.

**Emotional Triggers and Responses**:

- **Understanding Emotional Triggers**: Certain situations or experiences can trigger strong emotional responses. For example, feeling criticized may trigger anger or defensiveness, while feeling appreciated might lead to greater cooperation. By identifying what triggers specific emotions in you, you can gain a deeper understanding of your behavior and how to manage your emotional responses more effectively.
- **Emotional Regulation**: Part of understanding your behavior is learning how to regulate your emotions. This doesn't mean suppressing feelings but finding healthy ways to manage and express them. Emotional regulation skills help you pause before reacting impulsively, allowing for more thoughtful and balanced actions.

# 3. Understanding the Influence of Your Beliefs and Values

Your beliefs and values act as the lens through which you interpret the world. They shape how you respond to situations, make decisions, and interact with others. For example, if you believe that hard work always leads to success, you may be more persistent in the face of challenges. On the other hand, if you have a belief that success is only for a lucky few, you might avoid putting in effort or feel discouraged when things don't go as planned.

**Core Beliefs and Their Impact**:

- **Self-Beliefs**: The way you view yourself greatly impacts your behavior. If you believe you are capable and deserving of success, you're more likely to take initiative and pursue opportunities. Conversely, if you struggle with self-doubt or feelings of inadequacy, you may hesitate to take risks or avoid situations where you might fail.
- **Cultural and Societal Beliefs**: Our beliefs are often influenced by the culture and society we grow up in. Cultural norms and societal expectations can affect our behavior, shaping how we think about success, relationships, or how we "should" behave in certain situations. For example, some cultures emphasize community and collaboration, while others might focus more on individual achievement.

# 4. The Impact of Past Experiences on Behavior

Our past experiences, especially those in childhood, have a lasting impact on how we behave as adults. The messages we received from our family, peers, and teachers, along with the situations we experienced, can shape our emotional responses, coping mechanisms, and even our social behavior.

**Influence of Childhood and Early Relationships**:

- **Attachment Styles**: The way we form attachments in early childhood can influence how we behave in relationships later in life. For instance, those with a secure attachment style tend to have healthy, trusting relationships, while those with an insecure attachment style may struggle with fear of abandonment or difficulty trusting others.

- **Trauma and Past Wounds**: Early traumatic experiences, such as abuse, neglect, or loss, can leave deep emotional scars. These experiences might manifest in adult behavior through anxiety, defensive mechanisms, or difficulty trusting others. Understanding how past experiences influence your present actions is key to healing and changing harmful behaviors.

## 5. Social and Environmental Influences on Behavior

Human behavior is not only shaped by internal factors but also by external circumstances, including social influences and environmental factors. Our behavior often reflects the roles we take on in society, the relationships we have, and the settings we are in.

**The Role of Social Norms**:

- Social norms and expectations play a powerful role in shaping how we behave in different settings. We may act differently at work, with friends, or in family settings based on the expectations of those around us. Recognizing when your behavior is driven by external pressures rather than your authentic self can help you better align your actions with your true desires and values.

**Peer Influence and Group Dynamics**:

- The people around us have a strong influence on our behavior, whether we are aware of it or not. Peer pressure, groupthink, and social dynamics can push us to act in ways that we might not otherwise choose. For example, if you're in a group where everyone values success above all else, you might start prioritizing work over personal relationships, even if that goes against your core values.

## 6. Behavioral Triggers: Why We Act the Way We Do

Behavior is often driven by triggers—specific situations, emotions, or thoughts that prompt a particular action. Recognizing your triggers allows you to respond more mindfully rather than reacting automatically.
**Identifying Your Triggers**:

- Triggers can be external (e.g., a stressful work deadline, an argument with a loved one) or internal (e.g., negative self-talk, feelings of inadequacy). By becoming aware of your triggers, you can develop strategies for managing your reactions and making more intentional choices.

**Breaking the Reaction-Pattern Cycle**:

- When you are triggered, your brain often defaults to a habitual response. For example, if you get anxious before public speaking, you might avoid opportunities to speak in front of others. However, once you recognize this reaction pattern, you can consciously choose to face your fear and gradually build new responses.

Understanding your own behavior is an ongoing process that requires self-reflection, patience, and openness. By becoming more aware of the factors influencing your actions—whether internal beliefs, emotions, past experiences, or social influences—you can take greater control over your life and align your behavior with your goals, values, and true potential.

**Tools and Strategies for Increasing Self-Awareness**

Self-awareness is one of the most powerful tools for personal development.

It allows you to understand your thoughts, emotions, and behaviors, giving you the ability to recognize patterns, make better decisions, and improve your relationships. Building self-awareness isn't always easy, but there are a variety of tools and strategies that can help you gain deeper insights into yourself. By integrating these practices into your daily routine, you can become more attuned to your inner world and take intentional steps toward positive growth.

# 1. Mindfulness Practices

Mindfulness is the practice of being present in the moment, observing your thoughts, feelings, and sensations without judgment. It helps you become more aware of your internal experiences and reactions, allowing you to respond thoughtfully rather than react impulsively.

**Mindfulness Techniques**:

- **Breathing Exercises**: Simple breathing exercises can help you focus on the present moment. One common practice is to inhale for a count of four, hold for four, and exhale for four. This practice brings your attention to your breath, calming the mind and grounding you in the now.
- **Body Scanning**: This involves paying attention to different parts of your body from head to toe, noticing any tension or discomfort. Body scanning can reveal unconscious stress or emotions, which may be linked to certain behaviors or patterns.
- **Mindful Observation**: Take a few minutes each day to sit quietly and observe your surroundings without distraction. Focus on your senses— what you see, hear, smell, and feel. This can help you become more aware of your surroundings and how you react to them.

# 2. Journaling for Reflection

Writing down your thoughts, feelings, and experiences is one of the most effective ways to increase self-awareness. Journaling allows you to process your emotions, track your behaviors, and reflect on how your experiences shape your actions. Over time, journaling can help you recognize patterns in your behavior and uncover the underlying causes of your reactions.

**Types of Journaling Practices**:

- **Daily Reflection**: Write about your day, focusing on significant events, how you felt, and how you reacted. Reflect on what went well and what didn't, and ask yourself why you responded the way you did. Over time, this can help you identify recurring emotional responses or triggers.
- **Gratitude Journaling**: This practice involves listing things you're grateful for each day. It encourages a positive mindset and can help you identify the things in life that bring you joy, fulfillment, and contentment. By regularly noting the positives, you can shift your focus away from negativity and develop a greater sense of self-awareness.
- **Prompted Journaling**: Use prompts to dive deeper into your thoughts and feelings. Some examples of journaling prompts include: "What is something I'm avoiding?" "How do I feel about my current relationships?" or "What is one thing I would change about my behavior today?"

# 3. Feedback from Others

Often, we are too close to our own behavior to see it objectively. Getting feedback from trusted friends, family, or colleagues can provide valuable insights into how others perceive your actions and reactions. It can help you uncover blind spots in your self-awareness and encourage personal growth.

**Ways to Seek Feedback**:

- **Ask Open-Ended Questions**: When seeking feedback, ask questions like, "How do I come across in meetings?" or "Is there something I could do to improve our relationship?" Open-ended questions invite thoughtful responses and allow the other person to provide honest and constructive feedback.

- **Be Receptive to Criticism**: It's important to approach feedback with an open mind. Rather than becoming defensive, listen carefully to what others say, reflect on their comments, and use them as opportunities for growth. Remember that feedback is a tool for self-improvement, not a personal attack.
- **360-Degree Feedback**: In a professional context, 360-degree feedback involves receiving input from multiple sources—supervisors, colleagues, and direct reports. This approach provides a well-rounded view of your behavior and can highlight areas for improvement that you may not have considered.

## 4. Meditation and Visualization

Meditation and visualization are powerful tools for self-awareness. Meditation helps you quiet the mind, reducing distractions and allowing you to tune into your thoughts and feelings more clearly. Visualization techniques can help you imagine how you want to show up in certain situations and align your behavior with your desired outcomes.

**Meditation Practices**:

- **Guided Meditation**: Use audio or apps that guide you through meditation exercises. These can focus on areas such as stress relief, self-compassion, or body awareness. Many guided meditations help you observe your thoughts and feelings without getting caught up in them.
- **Loving-Kindness Meditation**: This practice involves focusing on cultivating feelings of love and compassion, first toward yourself and then toward others. It can increase your emotional awareness and help you connect more deeply with your feelings and intentions.
- **Breath-Focused Meditation**: Focusing on your breath while meditating can help you gain insight into your thought patterns and emotional states.

It helps create space between your thoughts and actions, giving you more control over how you respond to different situations.

# 5. Self-Assessment Tools

Self-assessment tools such as personality tests, strengths assessments, or emotional intelligence surveys can provide valuable insights into your behavioral tendencies, preferences, and emotional responses. These tools can help you better understand your motivations, identify your strengths, and pinpoint areas for growth.

**Common Self-Assessment Tools**:

- **Personality Assessments**: Tools like the Myers-Briggs Type Indicator (MBTI) or the Big Five Personality Traits can help you identify your personality traits and tendencies, such as whether you lean more toward introversion or extroversion, and how you process information and make decisions.
- **Strengths Finder**: The StrengthsFinder assessment identifies your core strengths, helping you understand where you excel and how to leverage those strengths in different areas of your life.
- **Emotional Intelligence (EI) Tests**: Emotional intelligence assessments help you gauge how well you recognize, understand, and manage your emotions, as well as how effectively you empathize with others. This can provide insight into your emotional self-awareness and social skills.

# 6. Observation and Reflection in Everyday Life

The way you react in everyday situations—whether it's during conversations, stressful moments, or when interacting with family and friends—can provide a wealth of information about your behavior and emotional patterns.

**Observing Your Reactions**:

- **Notice Patterns in Your Behavior**: Pay attention to how you react in different situations. Do you tend to get defensive when criticized? Do you withdraw from conflict or seek to please others? Recognizing these patterns can help you understand why you act the way you do in specific contexts.

- **Record Your Observations**: Keep a mental or physical log of your reactions in various situations. Over time, this can help you identify triggers, habitual responses, and areas where you may need to make changes.
- **Ask Yourself "Why?"**: When you feel a strong reaction to a situation, ask yourself why you're feeling that way. Is it based on past experiences, assumptions, or current emotions? Understanding the root cause of your feelings can help you gain greater self-awareness and make intentional changes in your behavior.

By consistently using these tools and strategies, you can develop a deeper understanding of your thoughts, emotions, and behaviors. This heightened self-awareness will empower you to make more conscious choices, break free from negative patterns, and create meaningful changes in your life.

## The Role of Reflection in Personal Development

Reflection is a powerful tool in personal development, allowing you to gain deeper insights into your thoughts, emotions, actions, and life experiences. It is the process of looking back on past experiences, analyzing them, and considering how they shape your current behavior, beliefs, and decisions. Through reflection, you can uncover valuable lessons, identify areas for growth, and develop a greater understanding of yourself. Whether through journaling, meditation, or conversations with others, reflection provides a structured way to pause, assess, and evolve in a mindful way.

# 1. Gaining Insight into Patterns of Behavior

One of the most significant benefits of reflection is the ability to recognize patterns in your behavior. We often engage in automatic behaviors or make decisions without fully considering the reasons behind them. By reflecting on your actions and decisions, you can identify recurring patterns and understand the driving forces behind your choices.

**How Reflection Uncovers Patterns**:

- **Identifying Triggers**: Reflection allows you to pinpoint what triggers certain behaviors, whether it's stress, fear, or external pressures. For example, if you frequently react with frustration in certain situations, reflecting on past occurrences can help you identify common threads—whether it's a specific person, context, or emotional state that sets off your reactions.
- **Recognizing Habits**: Regular reflection helps you recognize both positive and negative habits that may be influencing your life. For example, you might realize that procrastination occurs every time you feel overwhelmed by a task, or that you tend to overcommit to others out of a desire to avoid confrontation. Recognizing these patterns gives you the opportunity to address them consciously and make changes where needed.

# 2. Learning from Past Experiences

Reflection allows you to turn past experiences—whether successes or failures—into opportunities for growth. Instead of merely moving on from events, reflecting on them helps you extract lessons that can inform future decisions and actions.

**Key Areas of Learning through Reflection**:

- **Mistakes and Failures**: Reflecting on your mistakes allows you to gain a deeper understanding of what went wrong, why it happened, and what you can do differently next time. Rather than seeing failure as something to avoid, you can reframe it as a learning experience that offers valuable lessons for future success.

- **Successes and Strengths**: Reflection isn't just for analyzing mistakes; it's equally important for recognizing and celebrating successes. Reflecting on what went well and why you succeeded can reinforce positive behaviors and boost confidence. It allows you to see the strategies, strengths, and attitudes that led to success, making it easier to repeat those actions in the future.

- **Personal Growth**: Through reflection, you can assess how much you've grown over time. You may realize that, while you've faced challenges, you've also developed new skills, attitudes, and perspectives. Reflection helps you track this growth, which reinforces your sense of progress and motivates further self-improvement.

# 3. Gaining Clarity on Values and Goals

Reflection helps you align your actions with your core values and long-term goals. By pausing to think about what truly matters to you, you can ensure that your decisions are guided by your principles, rather than fleeting desires or external pressures.

**How Reflection Supports Goal Clarity:**

- **Clarifying Priorities**: When you reflect on your life and what's important to you, it becomes easier to identify your priorities. You may find that some of your past actions were not aligned with your true values, such as spending too much time on tasks that don't bring you fulfillment. Reflection allows you to recalibrate and make intentional choices that align with your core values.

- **Evaluating Progress**: Reflecting on your goals and progress helps you assess whether you are on track to achieve what you set out to do. It also provides an opportunity to reassess your goals, considering whether they are still relevant or if they need to be adjusted based on changing circumstances or new insights.

- **Creating Intentional Change**: Once you've identified what matters most to you, reflection helps you create an actionable plan for change. If you feel that your current life is not aligned with your values, reflection can help you understand the changes you need to make in order to live more authentically.

## 4. Enhancing Emotional Intelligence

Emotional intelligence (EQ) refers to the ability to recognize, understand, and manage your emotions, as well as the emotions of others. Reflection plays a key role in enhancing your EQ, as it encourages you to pause and examine how your emotions influence your actions and interactions.

**Emotional Awareness Through Reflection**:

- **Understanding Emotional Triggers**: By reflecting on your emotional responses in various situations, you can identify triggers that cause strong feelings, such as anger, anxiety, or joy. Recognizing these emotional patterns helps you understand why certain situations provoke intense reactions and how you can manage them more effectively.
- **Empathy and Relationships**: Reflection also helps you understand the emotional needs of others. By reflecting on your interactions, you can develop greater empathy and improve communication with others, leading to healthier and more productive relationships.

## 5. Building Resilience and Problem-Solving Skills

Reflection encourages resilience by helping you learn from difficult experiences and come up with strategies for overcoming future challenges. Instead of dwelling on obstacles or setbacks, reflection empowers you to find solutions, adapt to changing circumstances, and build mental toughness.

## Reflection as a Tool for Problem-Solving:

- **Looking at Challenges from Different Angles**: When you reflect on a problem or challenge, you can take the time to think through different solutions, weigh the pros and cons, and consider alternative approaches. This ability to think critically and problem-solve underpins your resilience in the face of adversity.
- **Learning from Past Difficulties**: Reflection helps you see how you've overcome past challenges, which reinforces your confidence in your ability to handle future ones. It allows you to recognize the strengths and strategies that helped you navigate difficulties, ensuring that you're better prepared for similar challenges in the future.

Reflection is an ongoing practice that can significantly enhance your personal development. By regularly taking time to assess your behaviors, emotions, and experiences, you can gain deeper insights into who you are, why you act the way you do, and how you can evolve. As you continue to engage in self-reflection, you'll build a stronger sense of self-awareness and become more intentional in your actions, leading to a more fulfilling and purpose-driven life.

# Chapter 10: The Influence of Society on Behavior

## How Culture and Society Shape Our Actions

Our behavior is not only influenced by personal experiences, internal drives, or biological factors, but also by the broader cultural and societal contexts in which we live. Culture and society provide the frameworks within which we learn how to behave, interact with others, and make decisions. These external influences shape everything from our values and beliefs to the way we express emotions, navigate social roles, and interpret the world around us. Understanding how culture and society shape our actions helps us gain insight into how we function as individuals within a collective, and how we can adapt or challenge certain societal norms and expectations.

## 1. The Influence of Cultural Norms and Values

Culture refers to the shared beliefs, customs, practices, and behaviors that are common within a particular group of people. Every culture has its own set of norms and values, which act as unwritten rules for how individuals within that culture are expected to behave. These cultural values influence everything from communication styles to social hierarchies, work ethics, and relationship dynamics.

**Cultural Norms and Behavior**:

- **Social Behavior and Etiquette**: In different cultures, what is considered polite or respectful behavior can vary greatly. For example, in many Western cultures, maintaining eye contact is seen as a sign of confidence and engagement, while in some Asian cultures, it might be considered rude or confrontational. These cultural norms shape how we interact with others and the expectations we have of ourselves and those around us.

- **Individualism vs. Collectivism**: One of the most significant ways culture shapes behavior is through the lens of **individualism** and **collectivism**. In individualistic cultures (e.g., the United States or many European countries), personal freedom, autonomy, and individual achievement are highly valued. People are encouraged to assert themselves, pursue personal goals, and prioritize their own needs and desires. In contrast, collectivist cultures (e.g., many Asian and Latin American cultures) place a stronger emphasis on community, family, and group harmony. In these societies, people are often expected to put the needs of the group before their own individual desires, and behaviors that disrupt group cohesion may be frowned upon.

- **Collective Identity**: Culture also shapes our sense of identity, including the roles we take on in society (e.g., as a student, parent, worker, or leader). These roles are guided by cultural expectations, and individuals often feel compelled to align their actions with what is culturally acceptable. For example, in some cultures, there may be strong pressure to conform to traditional gender roles, which can influence career choices, relationship dynamics, and parenting styles.

## 2. Socialization and the Transmission of Values

From the moment we are born, we are socialized into the cultural norms and values of our society. Socialization is the process through which we learn and internalize the behaviors, customs, and beliefs that are considered acceptable or desirable in our culture. This process starts within the family and extends to educational systems, peer groups, and broader societal institutions.

**Key Agents of Socialization**:

- **Family**: The family is often the first place where we learn social norms, values, and behaviors. Parents and caregivers influence early development by teaching us right from wrong, acceptable behaviors, and cultural practices. For instance, how we interact with authority, share resources, or approach conflict resolution is often shaped by our family environment.

- **Education**: Schools play a major role in socializing young people. In addition to academic learning, schools instill cultural values such as respect for authority, the importance of hard work, and social cooperation. Through interactions with teachers and peers, students learn about societal expectations and develop their social identities.

- **Media and Technology**: Television, social media, and other forms of mass communication also significantly impact behavior by shaping perceptions of reality. The media often reinforces cultural norms, such as beauty standards, gender roles, or consumer behavior, influencing how people behave or how they feel about themselves and others.

# 3. Social Pressure and Conformity

Society often exerts pressure on individuals to conform to certain expectations, which can strongly influence behavior. Social conformity is the act of adjusting one's behavior, beliefs, or attitudes to align with those of the group or society at large. Conformity can arise in various settings, such as in peer groups, workplaces, or larger cultural contexts.

**The Role of Social Pressure**:

- **Peer Influence**: Peer groups, particularly during adolescence, have a powerful influence on behavior. Young people often adopt behaviors and attitudes to fit in or gain acceptance from their peers, even if these actions go against their personal beliefs. For example, peer pressure can encourage behaviors like smoking, drinking, or adopting certain fashion styles.

- **Social Expectations**: Society also sets expectations for how we behave in different roles—whether as a parent, employee, student, or citizen. These expectations can shape decisions, such as whether to pursue certain careers, whether to marry or have children, or even how to express emotions. People often make choices based on societal norms, sometimes even at the cost of their own desires or aspirations.

- **Social Identity**: Social identity theory suggests that people tend to define themselves based on the groups to which they belong—be it nationality, religion, gender, or social class. These group identities can shape behaviors, as individuals may act in ways that reflect the values and norms of the group they identify with. For example, someone who strongly identifies with their cultural heritage might prioritize family gatherings, or someone involved in a political group may take actions aligned with the group's ideology.

## 4. The Impact of Social Institutions on Behavior

Social institutions, such as religion, government, and the legal system, also play a significant role in shaping how we behave. These institutions enforce rules and norms that dictate acceptable behavior, and they provide the structures that guide our actions in everyday life.

**Influences of Social Institutions**:

- **Religion**: Religious beliefs and practices influence behavior by promoting moral values, shaping ethical decisions, and guiding individuals in how they interact with others. For example, many religions promote compassion, charity, and kindness, while also setting guidelines for ethical behavior and personal conduct.

- **Law and Politics**: Legal systems dictate behavior by establishing rules that individuals must follow. Laws govern everything from traffic safety to criminal behavior, and the consequences of violating these laws can shape how people act. Political ideologies and systems of governance also influence societal behavior, as citizens often align their actions with political movements, policies, or national values.

- **Workplace Norms**: In professional settings, organizational culture and norms guide behavior. Workplace etiquette, performance expectations, and teamwork dynamics are all shaped by broader societal and organizational norms. For example, the emphasis on individual performance versus team success can vary depending on whether a society is more individualistic or collectivist.

In conclusion, culture and society shape our actions by providing the framework within which we learn, adapt, and live our lives. From our earliest experiences in family and education to the pressures of social conformity and the expectations of cultural and institutional norms, the influence of society is pervasive and powerful. By understanding how culture and society influence our behavior, we gain greater insight into our actions and can make more conscious decisions about how we want to engage with the world around us.

## Peer Pressure, Media, and Social Norms

Our behavior is heavily influenced by the people around us and the media we consume. Peer pressure, media representations, and societal norms all play key roles in shaping how we think, act, and present ourselves. These external influences often work subtly, reinforcing certain behaviors and expectations, and they can significantly impact our choices, values, and self-perception. Understanding how these forces affect our actions can help us make more informed decisions and resist pressures that don't align with our true selves.

# 1. Peer Pressure: The Influence of Those Around Us

Peer pressure refers to the influence exerted by a group of people—often our friends, classmates, colleagues, or social circles—to encourage us to adopt certain behaviors, values, or attitudes. While peer pressure is often associated with negative behaviors, such as engaging in risky activities, it can also have positive effects, such as encouraging people to pursue academic success or develop healthier habits.

**How Peer Pressure Shapes Behavior**:

- **Conformity to Group Expectations**: People naturally seek acceptance and belonging within their social groups. As a result, individuals may feel compelled to align their behaviors with those of their peers, even if these behaviors do not align with their personal values. For instance, a teenager might start smoking because their friends do, or someone might conform to a certain fashion trend because it's popular in their social circle.

- **Desire for Social Approval**: Peer pressure often works through the desire for social approval. People want to fit in, be liked, and be seen as "part of the group." This can lead individuals to adopt behaviors they wouldn't normally consider, whether it's engaging in certain activities, wearing particular clothes, or even adopting specific opinions or beliefs that align with the group. The fear of being ostracized or judged can push people to conform, even when it's against their better judgment.

- **Influence of Close vs. Distant Peers**: The influence of peers can vary based on how close or distant they are in the social hierarchy. Close friends or trusted family members often have a more significant influence because of the emotional connection and mutual trust. However, even distant or less-known peers can exert pressure, especially in environments like schools, workplaces, or social media spaces, where people are keenly aware of their social standing and reputation.

# 2. Media: Shaping Perceptions and Behavior

The media plays an undeniable role in shaping our understanding of the world, influencing our choices, and dictating cultural norms. Through television, social media, advertising, movies, music, and news, media creates powerful narratives about how we should look, behave, and live.

**The Role of Media in Shaping Actions**:

- **Advertising and Consumer Behavior**: Advertising often promotes ideals of beauty, success, and happiness through the products it endorses. Brands leverage powerful imagery and messages to persuade consumers that their products are necessary for social approval, status, or personal fulfillment. This can lead to consumerism, where people purchase products not necessarily out of need, but because media has convinced them it will enhance their social identity.

- **Social Media Influence**: Social media platforms, such as Instagram, TikTok, and Facebook, have a profound effect on how individuals perceive themselves and others. The curated nature of social media often promotes unrealistic standards of beauty, success, and happiness. People post idealized versions of their lives, which can lead to feelings of inadequacy or pressure to keep up with these portrayals. Social media also fosters a desire for validation through likes, comments, and shares, making people more likely to shape their behavior according to what will garner positive attention.

- **Body Image and Beauty Standards**: Media, especially television and advertising, has long been criticized for promoting narrow and unrealistic standards of beauty. The prevalence of photoshopped images, the glorification of particular body types, and the portrayal of unattainable beauty ideals have contributed to widespread dissatisfaction with personal appearance. These standards can affect self-esteem, leading people to engage in behaviors such as dieting, excessive exercise, or even plastic surgery to meet these ideals.

- **Influence of Celebrities and Influencers**: Celebrities and social media influencers often serve as role models or sources of inspiration. Their lifestyle choices, fashion preferences, and behaviors are often emulated by their followers. Whether through product endorsements, lifestyle content, or even their personal opinions, celebrities can shape societal trends, making their actions a form of peer influence on a larger scale.

# 3. Social Norms: Unwritten Rules of Society

Social norms are the unwritten rules and expectations that govern how people behave in a given society or group. These norms are learned through socialization and are influenced by culture, religion, history, and politics. While social norms can vary widely between cultures, they serve to maintain order and cohesion within a society.

**How Social Norms Influence Our Actions**:

- **Behavioral Expectations**: Social norms dictate how we should act in various situations—how we dress, speak, and behave in social interactions. For instance, norms about how to behave in formal settings (like a job interview or a wedding) differ greatly from how we behave in informal settings (like a casual hangout with friends). Failing to adhere to these norms can lead to social disapproval or exclusion, which drives people to conform.
- **Conformity and Social Pressure**: From a young age, individuals are taught to follow societal norms to gain acceptance. Whether it's through education, family teachings, or media, people learn what behaviors are acceptable and which ones are frowned upon. Nonconformity can result in judgment, ridicule, or even ostracism, which motivates people to act according to what society deems appropriate.
- **Cultural Shifts and Changing Norms**: Social norms are not static; they evolve over time as societies change. For example, norms surrounding gender roles, marriage, and career choices have shifted significantly in many parts of the world over the past few decades. While the pace of change can vary across different cultures, people's behaviors tend to

adapt to these shifting norms to remain socially aligned with their peers and communities.

- **Influence of Group Identity**: Norms also emerge from group identity, and the desire to belong to a particular group can strongly influence behavior. In some cases, people may engage in certain actions simply because it's the "norm" for their specific social or professional group. This is often seen in settings like workplaces, schools, or religious communities, where conformity helps individuals gain acceptance and reinforce their social standing.

In conclusion, peer pressure, media, and social norms shape our behaviors in both subtle and significant ways. While these influences can sometimes reinforce positive behaviors, they can also encourage actions that are out of alignment with our personal values and long-term goals. Becoming aware of how these external forces affect our choices can help us navigate societal pressures more consciously and make decisions that align with our true self.

## How to Resist Negative Influences

In a world filled with external pressures—from peer groups and social media to societal expectations—resisting negative influences can be challenging. These influences can sometimes push us toward behaviors, choices, or mindsets that are not aligned with our values, goals, or well-being. The ability to resist negative influences requires self-awareness, strong personal values, and practical strategies to stay grounded. Developing the skills to say no, make independent decisions, and maintain a healthy sense of self is essential for maintaining personal integrity and mental well-being.

# 1. Cultivate Self-Awareness

The first step in resisting negative influences is becoming aware of the ways in which they are affecting you. Self-awareness allows you to recognize when you're being swayed by external pressures and helps you understand the reasons behind your choices.

**Strategies for Building Self-Awareness**:

- **Reflection**: Take time to reflect on your actions and decisions regularly. Consider situations where you may have been influenced by others or by societal expectations. Ask yourself, "Did I make this decision because it aligns with my values, or was I trying to fit in?" This reflection helps you identify areas where you may be susceptible to negative influences and provides an opportunity for growth.
- **Mindfulness**: Practicing mindfulness can help you stay connected to your core beliefs and values in the present moment. By becoming more aware of your thoughts and emotions as they arise, you can avoid reacting impulsively to negative pressures.

# 2. Strengthen Your Personal Values and Beliefs

When you have a clear understanding of your values and beliefs, it becomes much easier to resist negative influences. People are less likely to sway you when you are confident in what you stand for and know what you want to achieve in life.

**Strategies for Strengthening Your Values**:

- **Clarify Your Values**: Take time to think about what is most important to you—whether it's honesty, kindness, health, financial independence, creativity, or another value. Write them down and remind yourself of them regularly to reinforce your commitment to living by these principles.
- **Set Clear Boundaries**: Having strong values helps you set boundaries

with others. When you know what you stand for, it's easier to assert yourself and say "no" to things that conflict with your principles. For example, if you value your health, you may resist peer pressure to indulge in unhealthy habits, such as excessive drinking or smoking.

- **Surround Yourself with Supportive People**: Building relationships with people who share similar values and respect your boundaries creates a positive environment that encourages your personal growth. Supportive friends and mentors can help you resist negative influences by offering encouragement and helping you stay accountable to your goals.

# 3. Learn to Say No

One of the most essential skills for resisting negative influences is learning to say "no" in a way that feels confident and assertive. Saying no doesn't have to be confrontational; it simply means setting boundaries that protect your values and well-being.

**Techniques for Saying No**:

- **Be Direct**: Instead of offering vague excuses or hesitating, be direct and firm. You don't need to over-explain yourself. A simple, "No, thank you, that's not something I'm interested in," can be enough.
- **Offer Alternatives**: If you feel comfortable, you can offer alternatives that align with your values. For example, if someone pressures you to skip exercise and go out for unhealthy food, you might suggest, "I'm going to go for a run instead, but maybe we can meet up after?"
- **Practice Saying No**: Like any skill, saying no gets easier with practice. Role-playing different scenarios in your mind or with a trusted friend can help you prepare for real-life situations. The more you practice, the more natural it will become to set boundaries and protect yourself from negative influences.

# 4. Develop Critical Thinking Skills

Critical thinking is the ability to analyze information, evaluate arguments, and make decisions based on evidence rather than emotional reactions or societal pressures. Developing critical thinking helps you question external influences and make more informed, rational decisions.

**Strategies to Strengthen Critical Thinking**:

- **Question Assumptions**: When you are exposed to a certain influence—whether it's from friends, the media, or advertising—ask yourself, "Why is this being presented to me? What is the agenda behind this message?" By questioning assumptions, you can better assess whether the influence aligns with your values and goals.
- **Weigh the Consequences**: Consider the potential consequences of your actions before making decisions. Ask yourself, "How will this choice affect my long-term goals?" This helps you evaluate whether the pressure to conform to a certain behavior is worth the potential negative outcomes.
- **Seek Diverse Perspectives**: Broaden your understanding by seeking information from multiple sources and viewpoints. Exposing yourself to different perspectives helps you develop a more balanced and informed opinion, which can make it easier to resist negative influences.

# 5. Manage Stress and Build Emotional Resilience

Often, negative influences can take hold when we are under stress or emotional pressure. People are more susceptible to external pressures when they feel anxious, insecure, or overwhelmed. Developing emotional resilience and stress-management techniques can help you stay grounded and make decisions that align with your long-term well-being.

**Techniques for Building Emotional Resilience**:

- **Mindfulness and Meditation**: Practicing mindfulness can help you stay present and centered, especially during times of stress. Meditation, breathing exercises, and relaxation techniques can reduce anxiety and improve your emotional regulation, helping you resist impulsive decisions based on external pressures.

- **Self-Care**: Taking care of your physical and mental health can strengthen your sense of self and make it easier to stand firm against negative influences. Prioritize regular exercise, healthy eating, and adequate sleep to improve your overall resilience.

- **Build a Support Network**: Having a group of supportive friends, family members, or mentors who encourage your personal growth can provide a buffer against negative influences. Surrounding yourself with people who understand your values and goals makes it easier to resist pressures from others.

# 6. Practice Self-Compassion

In the face of negative influences, it's easy to feel guilty, anxious, or inadequate when we don't conform to expectations. However, practicing self-compassion—treating yourself with kindness and understanding—helps you navigate difficult situations without beating yourself up.

**How Self-Compassion Helps**:

- **Forgiveness**: If you do give in to a negative influence, practicing self-compassion allows you to forgive yourself without harsh judgment. Understand that no one is perfect, and mistakes are part of the learning process.

- **Non-judgmental Awareness**: Self-compassion involves acknowledging your emotions and experiences without judgment. Instead of criticizing yourself for feeling weak or pressured, accept that it's natural to face challenges, and focus on how you can grow from the experience.

Resisting negative influences requires a combination of self-awareness, assertiveness, critical thinking, and emotional resilience. By strengthening these skills, you can build the confidence and independence needed to make choices that align with your true values and long-term goals.

# How to Resist Negative Influences

In today's world, we are constantly surrounded by influences from peers, family, media, and society that can lead us to make decisions or adopt behaviors that don't align with our true selves or values. These negative influences can come in many forms: peer pressure, social media, cultural expectations, or even toxic relationships. Learning how to resist these influences is crucial for maintaining personal integrity, making choices that support your well-being, and staying focused on your goals. Below are some practical strategies to help you resist negative influences and stay grounded in your beliefs.

# 1. Strengthen Your Self-Awareness

Self-awareness is the foundation of resisting negative influences. When you are self-aware, you can recognize when an external influence is pushing you to act in ways that are inconsistent with your values. You are better equipped to make conscious decisions rather than reacting impulsively.

**Strategies for Building Self-Awareness:**

- **Mindful Reflection**: Regularly take time to reflect on your thoughts, emotions, and actions. Journaling can be a helpful tool for this. Ask yourself questions like, "Why did I act that way?" or "What motivated that decision?" By reflecting on situations where you felt pressured, you can identify patterns and triggers, which allows you to be more prepared in the future.

- **Identify Your Triggers**: Often, negative influences target specific vulnerabilities. It could be the desire for approval, the need to fit in, or a fear of missing out. By identifying what triggers your susceptibility to negative influences, you can develop strategies to counteract them.

## 2. Strengthen Your Core Values and Beliefs

When you are clear about your values and what you stand for, resisting negative influences becomes easier. Knowing who you are and what you believe in gives you a solid foundation to make decisions that reflect your true self, even when external pressures are strong.

**Strategies for Strengthening Your Core Values**:

- **Clarify Your Values**: Spend some time defining your values and what is truly important to you. These might include things like honesty, respect, kindness, or health. When you have a clear understanding of your personal values, you can measure potential decisions against them. If a situation or influence conflicts with your values, you'll have a clearer sense of how to respond.
- **Create a Personal Mission Statement**: Write down a personal mission statement or a set of guiding principles that reflect your core beliefs. This written document serves as a reminder of who you are and what you stand for when you feel pressured to make choices that may not align with your values.

## 3. Build Confidence in Your Decisions

When you're confident in yourself and your decisions, you're less likely to be swayed by negative influences. Confidence comes from knowing that you are making choices that align with your values, goals, and self-respect.

**Strategies for Building Confidence**:

- **Start Small and Build Up**: Begin by practicing saying no to small, low-stakes situations where you feel pressured. For example, if a friend encourages you to skip a workout or eat unhealthy food, start by practicing the confidence to say no. These small wins help you build trust in your ability to resist bigger pressures in the future.
- **Visualize Positive Outcomes**: Before facing a situation where you feel pressured, take a moment to visualize yourself making the decision that aligns with your values. Imagine the positive feelings you'll have afterward, such as a sense of pride or self-respect. This visualization can help you make decisions with more conviction.

## 4. Surround Yourself with Supportive People

The people you surround yourself with play a significant role in the choices you make. If you are regularly exposed to negative influences, it's important to seek out supportive, positive people who share your values and encourage you to make decisions that are in your best interest.

**Strategies for Building a Supportive Network**:

- **Choose Relationships Wisely**: Evaluate the relationships in your life. Are they uplifting and supportive, or do they reinforce negative behaviors and pressures? Cultivate relationships with people who encourage you to grow, be yourself, and stay true to your values.
- **Find Mentors or Role Models**: Mentors or role models can provide valuable guidance when facing difficult decisions or external pressures. Seek out individuals who exemplify the kind of behavior you admire, and turn to them for advice when you feel unsure or influenced by negative pressures.

# 5. Learn to Say No

One of the most powerful ways to resist negative influences is simply to say no. Saying no allows you to set boundaries and protect your values, time, and well-being. It may feel uncomfortable at first, but with practice, you'll become more confident in your ability to assert yourself.

**Strategies for Saying No**:

- **Be Direct and Assertive**: When faced with pressure to act in a way you don't want to, practice being clear and direct. For example, you can say, "I'm not comfortable with that" or "That's not something I'm willing to do." You don't have to provide lengthy explanations; a simple, assertive "no" is enough.
- **Offer Alternatives**: If you don't want to participate in an activity but still want to maintain the relationship, offer a respectful alternative. For instance, if you don't want to go out drinking with friends, suggest another activity like going for a hike or seeing a movie together.

# 6. Practice Emotional Regulation

Often, negative influences work by playing on our emotions—whether it's fear, guilt, or the desire to be accepted. Being able to regulate your emotions helps you stay grounded and make rational decisions, rather than succumbing to emotional pressures.

**Strategies for Emotional Regulation**:

- **Pause Before Responding**: When you feel pressured, take a moment to pause and breathe. This gives you time to process the situation, calm any emotional reactions, and make a thoughtful decision.
- **Reframe Negative Emotions**: If you feel guilty for saying no, reframe that emotion. Instead of feeling bad, remind yourself that saying no is an act of self-respect and that you are making choices that align with your long-term well-being.

# 7. Focus on Long-Term Goals and Consequences

Negative influences often push for short-term gratification, while positive decisions are aligned with long-term goals and values. Keeping your focus on the bigger picture can help you resist the temptation to give in to momentary pressures.

**Strategies for Focusing on Long-Term Goals**:

- **Set Clear Goals**: Having clear, defined goals for your personal, professional, and health-related aspirations can help you stay focused on what truly matters. When faced with external pressures, ask yourself, "Will this decision bring me closer to my long-term goals?"
- **Consider the Consequences**: Before giving in to a negative influence, think about the potential long-term consequences. Will it help you reach your goals, or will it derail your progress? Visualizing the impact of your decisions on your future can make it easier to resist negative pressures in the present.

Resisting negative influences is not about eliminating them entirely from your life, but about strengthening your inner resolve to stay true to yourself, even when external pressures try to sway you. By cultivating self-awareness, building your confidence, and surrounding yourself with supportive individuals, you can make decisions that align with your values and goals, leading to greater personal fulfillment and resilience in the face of external pressures.

# Chapter 11: The Path to Personal Fulfillment

## Aligning Your Actions with Your Values

Aligning your actions with your values is one of the most powerful ways to live a fulfilling and authentic life. Our values serve as a compass, guiding us in making decisions, setting goals, and navigating challenges. However, in the midst of daily pressures, societal expectations, and external influences, it can be easy to lose sight of what truly matters to us. When our actions are in harmony with our core values, we experience greater satisfaction, confidence, and inner peace. Conversely, when we act in ways that contradict our values, we may feel conflicted, dissatisfied, or disconnected from ourselves.

## 1. Identifying Your Core Values

The first step to aligning your actions with your values is to clarify what your core values actually are. Core values are the fundamental principles that guide your decisions and behaviors in life. These values reflect what you hold most dear—what is truly important to you.

**How to Identify Your Core Values:**

- **Reflect on Past Experiences**: Think about times in your life when you felt truly proud, fulfilled, or at peace. What was happening during those moments? What qualities or principles were you honoring at the time? For example, if you felt proud of a project at work, it might reflect your value of **creativity** or **achievement**. If you felt fulfilled after spending time with family, it could point to the value you place on **relationships** or **connection**.

- **Use a Values List**: Sometimes, we need a bit of help to clarify our values. Using a list of common values (e.g., integrity, loyalty, kindness, responsibility, honesty, compassion) can prompt introspection. You can highlight the values that resonate most with you and begin to narrow them down to your top three to five core values.

- **Observe Role Models**: Consider the people you admire most, whether they're family members, friends, or public figures. What qualities or behaviors do you respect in them? These traits might reveal the values that you subconsciously hold dear.

## 2. Make Conscious, Value-Based Decisions

Once you've identified your core values, the next step is to ensure your actions align with them. This can be challenging at times, as life often presents situations where it's easier to go along with the flow, make compromises, or choose convenience over authenticity. However, making conscious decisions based on your values will lead to a more fulfilling and authentic life.

**How to Make Value-Based Decisions**:

- **Evaluate Opportunities Against Your Values**: Before committing to new projects, relationships, or activities, ask yourself how they align with your values. Does the opportunity reflect the things that matter most to you? For example, if one of your core values is **health**, you might hesitate to take a job that requires constant travel or late-night work, knowing it could interfere with your well-being.

- **Use Your Values as a Filter**: When faced with tough decisions, use your values as a filter to weigh your options. For instance, if your values include **honesty** and **integrity**, it might help you decide whether to speak up about a difficult issue, even when it's uncomfortable. If one option seems to align more closely with your core values, that's likely the path you should take.

- **Take Responsibility for Your Choices**: Aligning your actions with your values means taking responsibility for your choices, even when they require sacrifices or stepping out of your comfort zone. Living according to your values can sometimes mean standing up for what's right or making decisions that aren't always popular, but it's essential for maintaining your authenticity.

## 3. Overcoming Challenges to Staying Aligned

While aligning your actions with your values is rewarding, it's not always easy. External pressures, fear of judgment, or emotional impulses can sometimes cause us to act in ways that contradict our core beliefs. Recognizing and addressing these challenges is crucial for maintaining alignment.

**How to Overcome Challenges**:

- **Practice Self-Compassion**: It's important to recognize that no one is perfect. There will be times when you slip up or act in ways that don't reflect your values. In those moments, practice self-compassion. Acknowledge the misalignment without harsh self-criticism, learn from the experience, and recommit to your values moving forward.
- **Create Boundaries**: Sometimes, the pressure to act in ways that contradict your values comes from external influences—whether from peers, family, or society. Setting clear boundaries with others can help protect your integrity. For example, if one of your values is **respect**, but you find yourself in situations where others consistently disrespect you, it may be necessary to distance yourself from those relationships or assertively communicate your boundaries.
- **Surround Yourself with Like-Minded People**: The people you associate with can either reinforce or challenge your values. Surrounding

yourself with individuals who share similar values or who support your personal growth can help keep you aligned. These relationships can act as a source of encouragement, inspiration, and accountability.

## 4. Integrating Values into Your Daily Life

Consistency is key when it comes to aligning your actions with your values. This means making small, everyday choices that reflect your core beliefs. The more you practice value-based actions, the more natural and effortless they become.

**Practical Ways to Integrate Values:**

- **Daily Affirmations**: Reinforce your commitment to your values by creating affirmations that remind you of what's most important to you. For example, if **honesty** is a core value, an affirmation might be, "I am committed to speaking my truth and being authentic in all my interactions."
- **Set Intentions**: Each day, set a specific intention that reflects your values. This could be something as simple as choosing to be more **patient** with others, **generous** with your time, or **focused** on your goals. Setting clear intentions helps you stay mindful and proactive in aligning your actions.
- **Track Your Progress**: Consider tracking your actions in a way that allows you to assess how well you're living in alignment with your values. This could be through journaling or using a habit-tracking app. Regularly reviewing your progress helps you stay accountable to yourself and adjust your behavior as needed.

## 5. Realigning When Necessary

Life is full of changes, and our values can evolve over time. It's important to periodically reassess your values and how well your actions align with them. If you find that your priorities have shifted or that you're no longer acting in ways that reflect your values, take the time to realign.

**How to Realign with Your Values**:

- **Periodic Reflection**: Set aside time every few months to reflect on your values and goals. Ask yourself if your current actions still align with your beliefs and aspirations. If they don't, think about what changes you can make to get back on track.
- **Be Open to Change**: As you grow and learn more about yourself, your values might evolve. Embrace this growth and allow yourself the flexibility to realign with new insights and experiences.

By actively working to align your actions with your values, you can create a life that feels more meaningful, authentic, and true to who you are. It requires commitment, self-awareness, and continuous effort, but the rewards of living in alignment with your values are profound.

# Creating a Life You Truly Want

Creating a life you truly want involves aligning your actions, goals, and habits with what you genuinely value and desire. It is about moving away from external expectations or pressures and taking ownership of the direction you want your life to take. While creating this life requires self-awareness, intentionality, and persistence, it is entirely within your power to craft a fulfilling, authentic, and meaningful existence. This process can be broken down into several key steps, from discovering your passions to overcoming obstacles and creating sustainable habits that bring you closer to the life you envision.

# 1. Clarifying What You Truly Want

Before you can create the life you truly want, it's important to clearly define what that life looks like. Too often, we get caught up in societal expectations or the lives of others and end up following paths that don't align with our true desires. Taking the time to reflect on your true wants and needs is the foundation for building a life that feels meaningful to you.

**Steps to Clarify What You Want**:

- **Reflect on Your Values and Passions**: What are the things that matter most to you? What do you feel passionate about? Think about what excites you, what brings you joy, and what gives you a sense of purpose. For example, if you value creativity, you may find fulfillment in a career or hobby that allows for artistic expression. If you value connection, building relationships with family and friends may be a central aspect of your desired life.

- **Imagine Your Ideal Future**: Take some time to visualize your ideal future. Imagine what your life would look like in 5, 10, or 20 years. Where are you living? What kind of work are you doing? How do you spend your days? What kind of people are you surrounded by? This exercise can help you clarify your aspirations and start creating a roadmap for achieving them.

- **Identify Non-Negotiables**: What are the things you absolutely cannot live without or the things that you deeply need in your life to feel fulfilled? These could be emotional needs (like trust and honesty), lifestyle needs (such as freedom or stability), or relational needs (like family, love, or community). Identifying these non-negotiables helps ensure that you design a life that truly reflects your core desires.

## 2. Setting Clear, Intentional Goals

Once you've gained clarity on what you want, it's time to translate your dreams into actionable goals. Creating a life you truly want doesn't happen overnight, but breaking down big dreams into clear, actionable steps makes them achievable. Setting intentional goals provides structure and focus, helping you move in the direction of your vision every day.

**How to Set Effective Goals:**

- **Be Specific and Measurable**: Vague goals, like "I want to be happy" or "I want a better life," are not helpful because they lack clear direction. Instead, be specific about what you want to achieve. For example, instead of saying "I want to be healthier," set a goal like "I will exercise 3 times a week and eat more vegetables."
- **Make Goals Achievable and Realistic**: While it's important to challenge yourself, it's equally important to set goals that are attainable within your current circumstances. Break larger goals into smaller, manageable steps that you can realistically accomplish. This prevents overwhelm and helps maintain momentum.
- **Set Deadlines**: Deadlines give you a sense of urgency and keep you focused on your goals. Without deadlines, it's easy to let important goals slip through the cracks. Make sure your deadlines are reasonable and allow for flexibility, but give yourself something to aim for.

## 3. Overcoming Fear and Limiting Beliefs

Fear and limiting beliefs are some of the biggest barriers to creating the life you truly want. Many people are held back by the fear of failure, fear of judgment, or the belief that they aren't capable of achieving their dreams. To overcome these obstacles, you must recognize and address them directly.

**Strategies for Overcoming Fear and Limiting Beliefs:**

- **Challenge Negative Self-Talk**: Pay attention to your inner dialogue.

When you catch yourself thinking negatively or doubting your abilities, pause and challenge those thoughts. Ask yourself, "Is this belief based on facts or assumptions?" Replace limiting beliefs with empowering ones that reflect your true potential.

- **Take Small Steps Toward Your Fears**: Often, fear arises from the unknown. By taking small, manageable steps toward what you fear, you gradually build confidence and reduce the anxiety associated with taking risks. For instance, if you're afraid of public speaking, start by speaking in front of small groups before progressing to larger audiences.
- **Reframe Failure as Growth**: Many people avoid pursuing their dreams because they fear failure. However, failure is often an essential part of growth. Instead of seeing failure as a setback, reframe it as an opportunity to learn and improve. Every successful person has encountered failure at some point—what matters is how you respond to it.

# 4. Building Habits that Support Your Vision

Creating a life you truly want is not just about setting goals—it's about developing the daily habits that support those goals. Sustainable success is built on small, consistent actions that align with your vision. By making positive habits a regular part of your routine, you reinforce your commitment to your goals and create the foundation for long-term change.

**Building Supportive Habits**:

- **Start Small**: Don't overwhelm yourself by trying to change everything at once. Begin with small, manageable changes that you can easily incorporate into your daily routine. For example, if your goal is to live a healthier life, start by adding 10 minutes of exercise to your day, then gradually increase it over time.
- **Create Routines and Rituals**: Creating daily or weekly routines can help you stay consistent and organized. If writing a book is one of your goals, set aside a specific time each day for writing. Having a ritual or routine around your goals makes it easier to stay on track, even when

motivation fluctuates.

- **Accountability and Support**: Share your goals with trusted friends or family members who can support you and hold you accountable. Having someone to check in with can provide motivation and keep you focused on your vision. Alternatively, you can join groups or communities that share similar goals and values.

## 5. Embrace Flexibility and Adaptability

While it's important to have a vision and clear goals, it's equally important to stay adaptable and flexible. Life often presents unexpected challenges, and the path to your dreams may not always be linear. Embracing flexibility allows you to adjust your approach when necessary and respond to changing circumstances without losing sight of your core vision.

**Ways to Stay Flexible**:

- **Learn to Adapt**: Be open to course corrections. If something isn't working, consider alternative strategies. Life rarely goes as planned, and sometimes the detours can lead to even better opportunities.
- **Maintain a Positive Attitude**: Keep a positive attitude when facing obstacles. Rather than seeing challenges as roadblocks, view them as opportunities for growth and learning. Resilience and optimism are essential traits for creating the life you truly want.

## 6. Take Inspired Action and Stay Consistent

Finally, creating the life you truly want requires more than just thinking about it—it requires taking inspired, consistent action. The process of manifesting your ideal life involves aligning your day-to-day activities with your long-term goals. Progress may be slow at times, but with perseverance and a steady commitment to your vision, you will move closer to the life you desire.

**Taking Inspired Action**:

- **Break Goals into Actionable Steps**: Large goals can feel overwhelming, but breaking them down into smaller tasks makes them more achievable. Set daily, weekly, and monthly objectives that push you toward your larger goal.
- **Celebrate Progress**: Even small victories deserve recognition. Celebrating your progress along the way will keep you motivated and remind you that you are making strides toward the life you envision.

Creating a life you truly want is an ongoing process, but by clarifying your values, setting intentional goals, and building habits that support your vision, you are well on your way to living a life filled with purpose, fulfillment, and authenticity.

# Long-Term Strategies for Growth and Happiness

Achieving lasting growth and happiness isn't something that happens overnight. It requires intentional effort, a willingness to learn, and the ability to stay adaptable in the face of life's challenges. Long-term growth and happiness come from a combination of cultivating positive habits, building resilience, setting meaningful goals, and maintaining a healthy balance between various areas of life. Here are some key strategies to create a path that supports sustained personal growth and lasting happiness.

# 1. Cultivate a Growth Mindset

A growth mindset—the belief that your abilities and intelligence can develop over time—forms the foundation for long-term success and personal growth. When you adopt this mindset, you're more likely to embrace challenges, learn from setbacks, and continue developing throughout your life.

**How to Foster a Growth Mindset**:

- **Embrace Challenges**: Instead of avoiding tasks that seem difficult, approach them as opportunities to learn and improve. This will help you build resilience and develop new skills.
- **Learn from Failures**: Instead of seeing failure as a negative outcome, treat it as valuable feedback. Understand that mistakes are part of the learning process, and use them to adjust your approach in the future.
- **Celebrate Effort, Not Just Results**: Acknowledge and celebrate your effort and perseverance, even if the outcome isn't exactly what you expected. This reinforces the idea that growth comes from consistent practice and learning.

# 2. Prioritize Emotional Well-Being

Sustaining long-term happiness requires emotional well-being, which is cultivated through healthy emotional habits and coping strategies. When you maintain emotional balance, you're better equipped to navigate life's challenges with resilience and joy.

**Ways to Support Emotional Well-Being**:

- **Practice Self-Compassion**: Treat yourself with kindness during difficult times. Self-compassion means being understanding when you struggle or make mistakes, rather than engaging in self-criticism or negative self-talk.
- **Build Emotional Awareness**: Regularly check in with your emotions. Practice identifying what you're feeling and why, without judgment. This

helps you gain better control over your emotional responses and can improve how you handle stress and conflict.

- **Develop Coping Strategies**: Develop healthy ways to cope with stress and negative emotions, such as exercising, journaling, meditating, or talking to a trusted friend. Having tools for emotional regulation can help you maintain a positive outlook, even during challenging times.

# 3. Set Meaningful, Long-Term Goals

Long-term goals provide direction and purpose. They help guide your decisions and actions, ensuring that you are moving toward a future that is meaningful to you. Setting clear goals enables you to stay focused, stay motivated, and experience a sense of accomplishment as you work toward them.

**How to Set Effective Long-Term Goals**:

- **Identify Your Values and Priorities**: Your long-term goals should align with what you truly value. For example, if you value personal growth and learning, your long-term goal might involve continuous education or acquiring new skills. If you value family, a long-term goal could focus on spending quality time together.
- **Break Down Large Goals**: Large, long-term goals can feel overwhelming. Break them down into smaller, achievable steps, which will make them feel more manageable and help you stay motivated. These smaller milestones allow you to track progress and adjust your approach as needed.
- **Review and Adjust Regularly**: Life is dynamic, and your goals may evolve over time. Regularly revisit your goals to ensure they still align with your values and adjust them as needed based on your growth or changing circumstances.

# 4. Build Strong Relationships and Connections

Strong, supportive relationships are fundamental to happiness and personal growth. Relationships with family, friends, mentors, and colleagues provide emotional support, shared experiences, and opportunities for learning. Cultivating healthy, positive relationships helps create a sense of belonging and fulfillment.

**How to Build and Maintain Meaningful Relationships:**

- **Invest Time in Others**: Building lasting relationships requires time and effort. Make it a priority to connect with the people who matter most in your life. Spend quality time together, listen actively, and show genuine interest in their well-being.
- **Nurture Empathy and Communication**: Healthy relationships are built on open communication and empathy. Take time to understand others' perspectives, express your thoughts honestly, and be open to compromise and understanding when conflicts arise.
- **Surround Yourself with Positive People**: The people you spend time with have a profound impact on your mindset and emotional state. Seek out relationships with individuals who support your growth, share your values, and encourage your happiness.

# 5. Practice Consistent Self-Improvement

Personal growth is a lifelong process, and maintaining momentum requires ongoing effort. Developing the habit of continuous self-improvement can ensure that you're always moving toward a better version of yourself.

**How to Practice Self-Improvement:**

- **Read and Learn**: Make learning a regular part of your life. Reading books, taking courses, or seeking out new knowledge will help you grow intellectually and professionally.
- **Challenge Yourself Regularly**: Push yourself to try new things and step

out of your comfort zone. Whether it's developing a new skill, exploring a new hobby, or taking on a challenging project, these experiences will help you grow in confidence and competence.

- **Self-Reflection and Feedback**: Regularly reflect on your actions and decisions, and be open to feedback from others. This practice helps you gain insight into areas for improvement and encourages continuous learning.

# 6. Maintain Balance Across Life Domains

True happiness comes from maintaining a healthy balance between different areas of life, including work, personal relationships, health, and recreation. Focusing on one area while neglecting others can lead to burnout, stress, and dissatisfaction.

**Tips for Achieving Balance**:

- **Set Boundaries**: Learn to say no when necessary, especially if you're overcommitting to work or social obligations. Setting boundaries helps protect your time and energy, allowing you to focus on what's most important.
- **Prioritize Well-Being**: Take care of your physical and mental health. Exercise regularly, eat a balanced diet, get enough sleep, and engage in activities that help you relax and recharge.
- **Create Time for Leisure and Enjoyment**: Make time for activities that bring you joy, whether it's spending time with family, pursuing hobbies, or simply relaxing. A balanced life includes moments of play and rest, alongside work and responsibilities.

By incorporating these long-term strategies into your daily life, you can build a foundation for sustainable growth and lasting happiness.

# Putting It All Together

## Key Takeaways

Understanding human behavior and creating lasting personal growth involves a combination of self-awareness, emotional regulation, and the ability to resist negative external influences. As we explore the factors that shape our actions, it's essential to recognize the role that emotions, motivations, and societal influences play in the choices we make. Here are the key takeaways from the journey of self-discovery, behavior change, and long-term happiness:

## 1. Self-Awareness is Essential for Personal Growth

- **Self-awareness** is the first step toward making meaningful changes in your life. By recognizing your strengths, weaknesses, emotions, and patterns of behavior, you can better understand your motivations and identify areas for improvement.
- Tools like mindfulness, journaling, and regular reflection are powerful ways to cultivate self-awareness. These practices help you pause, observe your thoughts and emotions, and take intentional action aligned with your values.

## 2. Emotions Are Strong Drivers of Behavior

- Emotions strongly influence how we think, act, and make decisions. Understanding the science of emotional responses and learning to manage emotions can lead to better decision-making, healthier relationships, and greater resilience.
- Emotional intelligence—being able to recognize, understand, and regulate your emotions—plays a vital role in shaping behavior. Practices like mindfulness and emotional regulation help create a balanced emotional life, leading to more stable and thoughtful actions.

## 3. Motivation is a Key Factor in Behavior Change

- Motivation fuels the actions we take and is either **intrinsic** (driven by internal factors such as personal satisfaction or passion) or **extrinsic** (driven by external rewards or pressures).
- Focusing on intrinsic motivation, such as pursuing meaningful goals or engaging in activities that bring you joy and fulfillment, leads to more sustainable and positive behavior changes.

## 4. External Influences Can Shape Our Actions

- **Peer pressure**, **media**, and **cultural norms** play significant roles in shaping our behaviors. These external influences can either encourage positive behaviors or push us toward decisions that don't align with our true values.
- Recognizing the impact of these influences gives you the power to resist negative pressures and make more independent decisions. Strengthening your personal values and beliefs will help you stay grounded and true to yourself in the face of external expectations.

## 5. Aligning Actions with Core Values Leads to Fulfillment

- Aligning your actions with your **core values** and personal beliefs is key to living an authentic life. When you consistently make decisions that reflect your values, you experience a sense of fulfillment and satisfaction that is deeply rooted in your true self.
- Identifying your values and taking intentional actions that honor them, whether in relationships, work, or personal goals, helps create a life that feels meaningful and aligned with your true purpose.

## 6. Long-Term Happiness Comes from Balance and Growth

- Lasting happiness and growth come from a combination of **emotional well-being**, **resilience**, and **continuous learning**. By practicing self-compassion, fostering positive relationships, and setting long-term goals that align with your values, you build a foundation for sustained happiness.
- **Personal growth** is a lifelong process, requiring flexibility and the ability to adapt to change. It involves both achievements and setbacks, but each experience offers valuable insights for continued development.

## 7. Resisting Negative Influences Requires Strength and Boundaries

- Resisting negative influences—whether from peers, media, or societal pressures—requires strong boundaries and the ability to make choices that align with your values. Strengthening self-awareness, understanding your values, and practicing assertiveness are key strategies for staying true to yourself.
- By cultivating a growth mindset and focusing on intrinsic motivations, you empower yourself to make decisions based on what is best for your

long-term happiness and well-being, rather than succumbing to external pressures.

## 8. Personal Development Is a Continuous Journey

- The path to self-improvement and happiness is not linear, and there will always be room for growth and development. Embracing a **growth mindset**—believing that you can continue to evolve and learn throughout your life—helps you stay motivated and open to new possibilities.
- Each step you take toward greater self-awareness, emotional intelligence, and value-driven decision-making contributes to a life that is not just successful, but also fulfilling and aligned with your true self.

In conclusion, creating the life you want and achieving long-term happiness requires intentional effort, self-reflection, and the courage to make choices that reflect who you are at your core. By aligning your actions with your values, cultivating resilience, and learning to manage both external influences and internal emotions, you lay the groundwork for personal fulfillment and lasting growth.

# Moving Forward with a Deeper Understanding of Yourself

As you continue the journey of personal growth, a deeper understanding of yourself becomes the foundation for meaningful change, success, and fulfillment. This process isn't a one-time event but rather a continuous evolution that requires introspection, openness to growth, and the ability to adapt. By building on the insights gained through self-awareness, emotional intelligence, and the exploration of your values, you can chart a path toward a life that aligns with your true self. Here are some key steps to move forward with greater self-understanding and enhance your personal development journey.

# 1. Commit to Continuous Self-Reflection

Self-reflection is an ongoing process that helps you stay connected to your thoughts, emotions, and actions. By regularly taking time to reflect on your experiences, you can gain deeper insights into how you respond to various situations and what drives your decisions.

**How to Integrate Self-Reflection into Your Life**:

- **Set Aside Time for Reflection**: Make self-reflection a daily or weekly practice. It can be as simple as journaling for 10-15 minutes about your day or writing down what you've learned from specific experiences.
- **Ask Thoughtful Questions**: To deepen your reflection, ask yourself probing questions like, "What did I learn from this experience?" or "Why did I react the way I did?" This helps you dig beneath surface-level thoughts and understand your internal motivations.
- **Be Honest and Compassionate**: Self-reflection requires honesty with yourself, but also compassion. Avoid harsh self-criticism and instead, look at your experiences as opportunities for growth and learning.

## 2. Align Your Actions with Your Core Values

One of the most powerful ways to understand yourself and move forward is to live in alignment with your core values. When you consistently act in a way that reflects your deepest beliefs, you create a life that feels authentic and fulfilling. This alignment leads to inner peace and confidence, as your actions are in harmony with your true self.

**Steps to Align Your Life with Your Values**:

- **Clarify Your Core Values**: Spend time identifying your core values—what truly matters to you. These could include family, honesty, health, creativity, financial security, or personal growth. Write them down and refer back to them as you make decisions.
- **Assess Your Current Life**: Look at the areas of your life where you may be out of alignment with your values. Are there areas where you're acting out of obligation or external pressure instead of genuine desire? Take steps to course-correct.
- **Make Conscious Choices**: As you move forward, make conscious decisions that reflect your values. This might involve saying no to things that don't align with what's most important to you or setting boundaries with people who push you away from your true self.

## 3. Embrace Vulnerability and Openness to Growth

Self-understanding often requires stepping out of your comfort zone and being open to change. Growth isn't always easy—it requires vulnerability, the willingness to make mistakes, and the courage to challenge old beliefs and habits.

**How to Foster Openness to Growth**:

- **Challenge Your Comfort Zones**: Growth happens when you stretch yourself beyond what feels familiar. Take on new challenges, try unfamiliar activities, and push yourself to learn new things. These experiences will provide you with deeper insights into who you are and what you're capable of.

- **Accept Imperfection**: Understand that you won't always get things right. Mistakes are part of the growth process. By embracing your imperfections, you build resilience and develop a more authentic relationship with yourself.

- **Seek Feedback from Others**: Sometimes, others can offer perspectives that we can't see ourselves. Be open to constructive feedback from trusted friends, mentors, or coaches. This can help you identify blind spots and encourage further personal development.

# 4. Set Meaningful and Purposeful Goals

A deeper understanding of yourself allows you to set goals that are truly meaningful and fulfilling, not just goals influenced by external expectations or societal pressures. When you set goals that are aligned with your core values and passions, you create a sense of purpose and direction that propels you forward.

**How to Set Goals that Align with Your True Self**:

- **Identify What Matters Most**: Before setting goals, take a step back and think about what you truly want to achieve in your life. These goals should be rooted in what brings you joy, fulfillment, and a sense of purpose.

- **Make Goals Specific and Actionable**: Break down larger goals into smaller, achievable steps. This makes your goals more manageable and ensures you're consistently making progress toward what matters most.

- **Review and Adjust Regularly**: As you evolve, so too should your goals. Regularly assess your progress, celebrate achievements, and be willing to adjust your goals as you grow and learn more about yourself.

# 5. Build Resilience and Adaptability

Life will inevitably present challenges, and the key to navigating them successfully lies in resilience—the ability to bounce back from setbacks and adapt to change. By developing emotional resilience and a flexible mindset, you can approach life's ups and downs with confidence and perseverance.
**How to Build Resilience**:

- **Focus on What You Can Control**: During tough times, focus on aspects of your life that you can control. This gives you a sense of agency and empowers you to make changes in your life, even when external circumstances are beyond your control.
- **Cultivate Optimism**: Practice looking for the silver lining in difficult situations. While it may not always be easy, maintaining a hopeful outlook helps you stay motivated and bounce back more quickly from adversity.
- **Learn from Challenges**: Each challenge offers a lesson. By viewing obstacles as opportunities for growth and learning, you can turn setbacks into stepping stones on your path to greater self-awareness and success.

# 6. Nurture Relationships that Support Your Growth

The people you surround yourself with play a significant role in your personal development. Positive, supportive relationships can uplift you, offer valuable feedback, and help you stay motivated. Nurturing these relationships is vital for your continued growth and happiness.
**How to Foster Positive Relationships**:

- **Surround Yourself with Like-Minded People**: Build a network of individuals who share your values and support your growth. These people encourage your personal development and challenge you to be your best self.
- **Set Boundaries**: Protect your energy and well-being by setting clear boundaries with people who may drain you or push you away from your

true self.

- **Practice Empathy and Communication**: Cultivate empathy in your relationships by listening actively and communicating openly. Building deep, understanding connections fosters trust and support, which are essential for personal growth.

# 7. Make Personal Development a Lifelong Journey

Personal growth doesn't have an endpoint; it's a lifelong journey. Embrace the process of self-discovery and continue to evolve as you encounter new experiences, challenges, and opportunities.

**How to Make Personal Development a Lifelong Commitment**:

- **Stay Curious and Open**: Never stop learning about yourself and the world around you. Stay open to new ideas, experiences, and ways of thinking that can help you grow.
- **Celebrate Progress, Not Perfection**: Acknowledge the progress you've made, even if it feels small. Personal development isn't about achieving perfection but about making continual, meaningful improvements.
- **Practice Patience**: Change takes time. Be patient with yourself and trust that growth is happening, even if it's not always immediately visible.

By committing to these steps, you can continue to deepen your understanding of yourself and create a life that aligns with your true values, passions, and aspirations.

# Final Words of Encouragement

As you move forward on your journey of self-discovery and personal growth, remember that the path to becoming the best version of yourself is not always linear. It is filled with ups and downs, moments of clarity and confusion, successes and setbacks. But with every step you take, you are growing, evolving, and becoming more in tune with who you truly are. The key is to remain patient, persistent, and kind to yourself along the way. Here are a few final thoughts to keep in mind as you continue your journey:

# 1. Progress, Not Perfection

Growth is not about being perfect—it's about progress. Every small step you take toward understanding yourself better, making healthier choices, or building stronger habits is a victory. Don't get discouraged by moments of failure or imperfection; they are part of the process. Embrace them as opportunities to learn, adjust, and improve. Remember, perfection is an illusion, but consistent progress leads to long-term success.

# 2. Embrace Change and Adaptability

Personal growth is all about change, and change can be uncomfortable at times. It's natural to feel uncertain when stepping outside of your comfort zone or challenging old beliefs and behaviors. However, the willingness to adapt and grow is what will ultimately allow you to create the life you want. Stay open to new experiences, new perspectives, and new ways of thinking. By embracing change, you open yourself up to endless possibilities and growth.

## 3. Be Compassionate with Yourself

The road to self-improvement requires self-compassion. Be patient with yourself when you slip up or when things don't go as planned. Understand that growth is a gradual process, and you will encounter obstacles along the way. Rather than being hard on yourself, treat yourself with the same kindness and understanding that you would offer a close friend going through a similar experience. Acknowledge your progress and celebrate the small wins.

## 4. Keep Your Vision in Focus

It's easy to get caught up in the day-to-day challenges and forget why you started. Keep your long-term vision and goals in mind, and let them be your guiding light. When things feel tough, remind yourself of your bigger purpose and the life you want to create. Revisit your core values, reflect on the person you want to become, and keep moving forward with determination.

## 5. Surround Yourself with Positive Influences

As you continue your journey of self-discovery, make sure to surround yourself with people and environments that uplift and support you. Positive influences can encourage you to keep going, help you stay grounded, and inspire you when you face challenges. Whether it's a supportive community, a mentor, or friends who share your values, having a network of people who believe in you can make all the difference in maintaining motivation and direction.

## 6. Trust the Process

Lastly, trust the process. Growth takes time, and the path to becoming the best version of yourself is not always predictable. There may be times when you feel stuck or uncertain, but remember that every experience, even the difficult ones, contributes to your development. Trust that each step, no matter how small, is bringing you closer to the life you truly want.

## Keep Moving Forward

As you move forward, know that you have everything you need to succeed within you. The courage to face challenges, the resilience to bounce back, and the wisdom to learn from your experiences are all part of who you are. Stay committed to your personal growth, trust in your journey, and remember that you are capable of creating a life that is authentic, fulfilling, and aligned with your true self.

Keep moving forward—step by step, day by day—and embrace the powerful, transformative journey that lies ahead.

# Appendix

In this section, we've compiled a variety of resources that can deepen your understanding of the concepts explored in "Understanding the Why Behind Our Actions." Whether you're interested in learning more about personality psychology, engaging in self-reflection exercises, or exploring tools for personal growth, these resources are designed to help you continue your journey of self-discovery and improvement.

## 1. Articles on Personality Psychology

Personality psychology is a vast field, and there is a wealth of information available that delves into the science behind how and why we behave the way we do. The following articles provide a deeper exploration of personality traits, how they develop, and their impact on our behavior:

- **"The Role of Genetics in Personality Development"**
- Explore how genetic factors shape our personalities, including the debate between nature and nurture in influencing behavior.
- *Source*: Verywell Mindhttps://www.verywellmind.com/
- **"How Personality Tests Help Us Understand Ourselves"**
- This article explains the purpose and utility of personality assessments, such as the Myers-Briggs Type Indicator (MBTI) and the NEO-PI-R, in identifying patterns in our behavior and preferences.
- *Source*: The Journal of Personality Assessment https://www.tandfonline.com/

- **"Understanding Emotional Intelligence and Its Role in Personality"**
- A comprehensive piece on the concept of emotional intelligence, how it shapes personality, and its influence on our relationships and decision-making.
- *Source*: Harvard Business Review https://hbr.org/

# 2. Worksheets and Exercises for Self-Reflection

Self-reflection is a powerful tool for gaining deeper insights into your behavior, thoughts, and emotions. Below are several worksheets and exercises designed to help you increase self-awareness, challenge limiting beliefs, and make intentional changes in your life.

- **Self-Reflection Journal Prompts**
- A list of daily or weekly journal prompts that encourage you to reflect on your actions, emotional responses, and goals. These prompts are designed to help you gain clarity on your motivations and identify areas for growth.
- *Example Prompts*:
- What is a recent situation in which I reacted emotionally? Why did I feel that way?
- What are my core values, and how did my actions align (or not align) with them today?
- What is one thing I can improve in my behavior moving forward?
- **The Wheel of Life Exercise**
- This exercise helps you assess your satisfaction in key areas of life (e.g., relationships, career, health, personal growth) and identify areas where you want to make changes or improvements. By visually mapping out where you stand in different areas, you can pinpoint where you need to focus your energy for a more balanced and fulfilling life.
- *Source*: MindToolshttps://www.mindtools.com
- **Personality Inventory Assessment**
- A worksheet designed to help you explore and assess your own personal-

ity traits, such as how you relate to others, how you make decisions, and your general attitudes toward life. This self-assessment encourages you to identify patterns and preferences that shape your behavior.

- *Example Questions*:
- How do I typically respond to stress?
- Do I prefer working alone or with a team?
- What motivates me to take action in different situations?
- **Strengths and Weaknesses Exercise**
- A reflective exercise that helps you identify your strengths and areas for improvement. Understanding these aspects of yourself can empower you to build on your strengths and address weaknesses constructively.
- *Instructions*:
- List your top three strengths and how you can leverage them in different areas of your life.
- List your top three weaknesses and consider small, actionable steps to improve in each area.

# 3. Recommended Tools for Personal Growth

The following tools and resources can help you continue your personal development, improve your emotional intelligence, and work toward your goals.

- **Mindfulness Apps**
- Mindfulness practice is essential for self-awareness and emotional regulation. These apps offer guided meditations and mindfulness exercises that can help you stay grounded and focused.
- **Headspace** – Offers guided meditations for stress relief, focus, and emotional well-being.
- **Calm** – Focuses on relaxation techniques, including guided breathing exercises, sleep stories, and meditation.
- **Insight Timer** – Features a wide variety of guided meditations, music, and talks to support mindfulness and personal growth.

- **Personality and Emotional Intelligence Assessments**
- To gain a deeper understanding of your personality and emotional intelligence, consider taking a professional assessment. These tests can offer detailed feedback that highlights your strengths and growth opportunities.
- **Myers-Briggs Type Indicator (MBTI)** – A well-known personality test that helps you identify your personality type based on your preferences in perception and decision-making.
- **The NEO Personality Inventory** – An in-depth test based on the Big Five personality traits that assesses how you score on dimensions like openness, conscientiousness, and emotional stability.
- **Emotional Intelligence 2.0** – A tool that assesses your emotional intelligence and provides strategies for improving your emotional awareness and regulation.
- **Online Courses and Workshops**
- Online courses offer a great way to dive deeper into specific areas of personal development. These platforms provide a range of learning opportunities from psychology basics to advanced emotional intelligence and growth strategies:
- **Coursera** – Offers courses in psychology, self-improvement, mindfulness, and emotional intelligence from top universities.
- **Udemy** – Features a wide range of personal development courses, including ones on self-awareness, leadership, and emotional mastery.
- **The Greater Good Science Center** – Based at UC Berkeley, this center offers resources and courses on emotional well-being, positive psychology, and resilience.

## Conclusion

The resources listed above are just a starting point for furthering your understanding of personality psychology, engaging in self-reflection, and exploring tools for personal growth. As you continue your journey toward a deeper understanding of yourself, remember that the most important step is the one you take today. Each small action you take to reflect, grow, and challenge yourself brings you closer to becoming the person you want to be. Use these resources to guide you, and don't be afraid to seek out new tools and ideas that will help you on your path to continuous growth and happiness.

# About the Author

Samuel Moore, PsyD, is a clinical psychologist, author, and passionate advocate for personal development. With over a decade of experience in the field of psychology, Samuel has worked with individuals from all walks of life, helping them navigate the complexities of their emotions, behaviors, and relationships. His unique approach combines evidence-based therapeutic techniques with a deep understanding of personality psychology, offering practical insights into the ways our actions are shaped by both internal and external factors.

Samuel's work is rooted in his belief that self-awareness and emotional intelligence are essential for creating meaningful change in one's life. Through his writing, he aims to make complex psychological concepts accessible to a broad audience, empowering readers to understand themselves better, overcome challenges, and build healthier, more fulfilling lives.

In addition to his clinical work, Samuel is a frequent speaker and educator, leading workshops and seminars on topics ranging from personal growth to conflict resolution. His passion for helping others unlock their potential is reflected in both his professional practice and his writings. When he's not working with clients or writing, Samuel enjoys spending time with his family, hiking in nature, and exploring the ever-evolving world of psychology.

# Also by Samuel Moore, PsyD

As a clinical psychologist with a PsyD, I specialize in helping individuals understand the underlying reasons behind their thoughts, emotions, and behaviors. My work focuses on combining practical therapeutic techniques with deep psychological insights to support personal growth, emotional well-being, and improved relationships. I use a variety of evidence-based approaches, including cognitive-behavioral therapy (CBT), mindfulness, and personality psychology, to help clients overcome challenges, build self-awareness, and achieve lasting change. Whether in therapy sessions or through my writing, my goal is to empower people to better understand themselves and create the lives they truly desire.

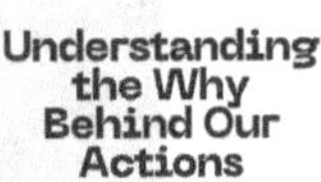

**Understanding the Why Behind Our Actions**

Dr. Samuel Moore is a clinical psychologist dedicated to helping individuals **Understanding the Why Behind Our Actions** With years of experience in personality psychology and emotional well-being, he combines therapeutic techniques with practical insights to guide people toward lasting personal growth. Whether through his work with clients or his writing, Samuel empowers others to build self-awareness, overcome challenges, and live more fulfilling lives.